To Stephen for research, support and a personal fitness programme.

MICHAEL COLEMAN

Illustrated by
Aidan Potts

Other titles to look out for:

Potty Politics

Galloping Galaxies

Murderous Maths

Foul Football

Scholastic Children's Books,
Commonwealth House, 1–19 New Oxford Street,
London WC1A 1NU, UK
A division of Scholastic Limited
London ~ New York ~ Toronto ~ Sydney ~ Auckland

Published by Scholastic Limited 1996

Text copyright © Michael Coleman 1996
Illustrations copyright © Aidan Potts 1996

ISBN 0 590 13753 0

Typeset by TW Typesetting, Midsomer Norton, Avon
Printed by Cox & Wyman Ltd, Reading, Berks

10 9 8 7 6 5 4 3 2 1

The right of Michael Coleman and Aidan Potts to be identified as the author and
illustrator of this work respectively has been asserted by them in accordance with
the Copyright, Designs and Patents Act, 1988.

Contents

INTRODUCTION

In July 1996, the Summer Olympic Games will be 100 years old. They first started in 1896, in Greece. In 1996 they will be held in Atlanta, USA.

So, let's start with a question. Why do you think this book has been called *Flaming Olympics*? Is it because:

- It's celebrating 100 years of Summer Olympics?
- Running tracks used to be made out of cinders?
- Lots of races are held in heats?
- The man who started the Olympics was a bright spark?

Sorry, if you've picked one of these, you're wrong!

Here's another four to choose from. Do you think this book is called *Flaming Olympics* because:

- There've been loads of scorching performances at the Olympics?
- There've been plenty of red faces at the Olympics?
- There've been lots of flashy characters at the Olympics?
- There've been dozens of blazing rows at the Olympics?

You've said "yes" to one of these? Now you're getting warmer! Over the one hundred years since the Olympic Games started again, there have been stacks of red-hot performances *and* stacks of red faces *and* stacks of flashy characters *and* stacks and stacks of blazing rows!

But none of these reasons are exactly why the book's called *Flaming Olympics*. So why is it? Check out the word "flame" in your dictionary. If you do, you'll see that one of its meanings is something like: *to become violently excited, passionate or angry.*

And *that's* why this book is called *Flaming Olympics*. It's because, of all the sporting occasions in the world, none has seen as many exciting, or passionate, or angry incidents take place as the Olympic Games.

They had plenty in the Ancient Olympics, which ran – well, staggered – from 776BC to AD394. We've had another 100 years of them since the modern Games started in 1896. In fact, there've been so many amazing incidents over the years, it's a wonder the Olympic Games haven't been re-named the Olympic *Fun* and Games.

And the best incidents from the Summer Olympics are all in this book! So, if you want to amaze your friends and wow your teachers with tales of:

- Flaming Olympic champs and Flaming Olympic chumps.
- Flaming Olympic tracks and Flaming Olympic tricks.
- Flaming Olympic disputes and Flaming Olympic disasters – then start reading!

THE FLAMING ANCIENT OLYMPICS

The Olympic Games aren't a new invention, you know. They've been around for well over 2,500 years – that's probably even before your teacher was born (although you might like to check to make sure)! They were first held in the Kingdom of Elis, in Greece, at a site called Olympia – which is how the word *Olympic* came to be used.

There are various tales about exactly how the Games began, but legend has it that they were the invention of a Greek hero called Heracles...

Heracles' Big Job

Now Heracles, or Hercules as he became more commonly known, was a sort of Greek version of Superman. He was supposed to be the son of Zeus, the Greek god in charge of thunder and lightning – a flaming Greek god if ever there was one! This might explain why Heracles was always having flashes of temper! One of his earliest occurred during a music lesson. Heracles objected to being told by his teacher that his lyre-

IS IT A BIRD? IS IT A PLANE? NO! IT'S **HERACLES !!!**

playing wasn't very good. So, what did he do? He swung his lyre and killed his teacher with one blow. (Was this pop music's first number one hit?)

After that, Heracles went on to kill a few other creatures – including a lion – until one day he killed some of his own children. This made the gods pretty angry and, although Heracles said he was sorry, they decided that wasn't enough.

Heracles was given twelve jobs to carry out as a punishment, a sort of super-detention. These jobs became known as the Twelve Labours of Heracles. One of them was for the King of Augea.

Heracles put on his best suit and turned up on time. He soon realised that putting on his best suit had been a bad move. The conversation went something like this...

How king-sized was Heracles' problem?
Can you do the sums?

3,000 oxen, doing 2 poos per day

= .... ox-poos per day

x 365 (for every day in the year, but
ignoring leap years) = ... ox-poos per year

x 30 (for every year since the stables
were last cleaned) = ... ox-poos all together!

But Heracles managed it. How? Simple. Instead of messing about with a mop and bucket, he used his super-powers to change the direction of two rivers so that they flowed right through the stables and out the other side. The water swept all before it (I'd hate to think where!), and the stables were cleaned.

And, so the story goes, "flushed" with success at how strong and quick he'd been, Heracles decided to celebrate by setting up a competition in which everybody else could see how strong and quick they were. He called this competition the Olympic Games, and dedicated them in honour of his father Zeus.

Flaming Festivals

However they really came about, the ancient Games were first and foremost a religious festival. That is, as well as the different sporting competitions, there was a lot of praying and sacrificing going on in honour of good old Zeus.

At first this just took one day. Then more events were added and they needed two days. Then more and more events were added, so that by 692BC the Olympics were lasting a full five days.

So, what went on? Here's an early programme (bought from an early programme-seller – yes, they had those, too).

15

OLYMPIC GAMES

TO BE HELD AT OLYMPIA IN THE KINGDOM OF ELIS
FOR THE HONOUR OF ZEUS

DAY 1
OPENING PROCESSION AND SACRIFICES TO ZEUS.
JUDGES' SWEARING AND ATHLETES' OATHS.
(BUT BAD LANGUAGE FROM SPECTATORS WILL NOT BE TOLERATED)

DAY 2
PENTATHLON·
POETRY AND ALL THAT CISSY STUFF·
CHARIOT RACES·

DAY 3
MORE SACRIFICES TO ZEUSS·
FOOTRACES·

DAY 4
RUNNING-IN-ARMOUR RACE · BOXING
WRESTLING · PANKRATION ·
(NOTE: SPECTATORS CAUGHT FIGHTING
WILL BE THROWN OUT·)

DAY 5
PRIZE-GIVING·
THANKSGIVING TO ZEUSS·
BANQUET FOR THE WINNERS·

Day 1: Promises, promises

On the opening day, the athletes all swore an oath to Zeus that they would play fairly.

The judges did the same, promising also that they would keep secret anything they learned about a competitor. (Unless they'd found out he'd been cheating! Then they had him whipped.)

Day 2: Fun and Games

The sporting events started on day two. A five-activity event came first. This was known as the Pentathlon, from the Greek word *pente*, meaning "five". In the pentathlon competitors had to throw the discus, throw the javelin, run, wrestle and jump – though not all at once of course.

WATCH IT MATE OR I'LL GIVE YOU A BUNCH OF PENTES!

The chariot races took place on the same day. They could be really gruesome. In every race you would see whips smacking against sweating flesh and hear the awful cries of creatures in agony – and that was just what the chariot drivers were doing to each other! The poor old horses had an even tougher time.

But even they didn't have as tough a time as the oxen on day three...

Day 3, morning: Noughts and Oxen

If you were going to take part in the ancient Games it was definitely NOT a good idea to be an ox. Why not?

- Because at the start of day three at every Olympiad, you and 99 other oxen would be slaughtered in honour of Zeus.
- You would then be cut up and your thighs burnt on the altar of Zeus in sacrifice (joining the pile of ox-thigh-ash at Olympia which, by the Second century AD, was over 6 metres high!).
- The rest of you would be cooked and eaten by the winning athletes at the big banquet which ended the Games.

Day 3, afternoon: Oh, My Foot!

After the oxo-cubing, it was time for the foot races. The shortest was the Stade, a straight race down the length of the arena – or "stadium" – as it came to be known because of its length. A stade measured the curious distance of 192.27 metres. Legends say that this measurement was also based on a supposed fact about Heracles. Was it:

- 60 times the length of Heracles' foot?
- The distance Heracles could walk in one breath?
- The distance Heracles could run in one breath?

IS THIS WHAT THEY CALL ATHLETES' FOOT?

Answer: There are legends suggesting all three. (Could they all be right? Maybe Heracles walked by putting one foot in front of the other, and because he was a bit of a thicko, he held his breath because he couldn't do two things at once, but because he was also a super-hero he did it so quickly the grounds-man thought he was running...)

There were two other foot-races: the *Diaulos* (of two stades, to the end of the stadium and back) and the *Dolichos* (of 24 stades). If you managed to win all

19

three of these races you were given the title *Triastes*, meaning "triple winner". One fabulous runner named Leonidas of Rhodes won this title four Games in a row (or should that be four Games running!)

Day 4: Perilous Pankration

Day four was not for the faint-hearted. Basically, it was punch-up day with wrestling and boxing leading up to the meanest, nastiest, toughest sport ever invented: *pankration*.

Pankration is a Greek word which is made from two other Greek words: *pan*, meaning "all", and *kratew* meaning "be strong, take hold".

So, what does *pankration* mean? "Strongest of all"? "Take hold of everything"? From the sound of what went on, both of them! Pankration was certainly an event for the strongest men. But it was also one in which you were allowed to grab hold of everything – and, as the fighters were naked, everything was definitely grabbable!

THAT WAS MY 'BELOW THE BELLY-BUTTON' SPECIAL!

PANKRATION
THE 10 OFFICIAL RULES
RULE 1. NO BITING
RULE 2. NO GOUGING
RULES 3-10 NO MORE RULES

That's it. In pankration you could do what you liked
to your opponent except bite him or put your thumb
in his eye and pull it out (your thumb *and* his eye).
The trouble was, of course, your opponent could do
the same to you! Also, unlike wrestling and boxing
nowadays, light and heavy fighters weren't
separated. They were put in against each other
(which was when the light ones *did* get separated –
usually from their arms and legs). There were no
rounds, either, for the fighters to take a breather. A
pankration match just went on and on until
somebody gave in, or dropped – dead if necessary.

Day 5: Prize-giving Day

For those who survived to see
it, day five of the ancient
Games was one of celebration.
A bit like a school Awards
Assembly, this was the day
when the prizes were given
out to the winners of the
different events.

And what were the prizes? At the Games
themselves, not much. Just an olive wreath and, if

you were brilliantly successful, the honour of having the Games named after you. Apart from that, most of the athletes waited until they got home before they cashed in. Olympic champions would then often be given money and good jobs, not asked to pay taxes – even be allowed to eat out free for life.

Could you have been a judge at the ancient Olympics?

At the ancient Olympics, judges had to be dead honest – otherwise they were likely to end up dead. See how you would have got on in this Ancient Olympic Quiz.

1. At the opening ceremony, you promise to be an honest judge. Do you show this by:
   a) signing an agreement
   b) saying you'll fall on your sword if you're not honest
   c) dipping your hands in blood

2. You've got to make sure all the runners in the foot race start from the same place. Do you:
   a) scratch a line on the ground and make them stand behind it
   b) stand in front of them, then get out of the way fast
   c) hold a javelin out in front of them until they get the point

SOMETIMES I HAVE TO BE BLUNT!

3. In the Pankration event (a mixture of Boxing and Wrestling), one man turns up with his fists bound in leather and covered in metal. Do you:
- a) disqualify him
- b) tell him to be a good boy and take it all off
- c) let the fight go on

4. It's the big Pankration final: Aggroppo the 'Ard versus Mangulon the Mad. Aggroppo grabs Mangulon's foot and twists it. Mangulon decides to have a go at strangling him.

Aggroppo twists Mangulon's foot a lot 'arder. But, just as Mangulon raises one arm to give in, he manages to finish strangling Aggroppo with his other arm. Aggroppo drops down dead. Do you:
- a) declare Mangulon the winner
- b) declare Aggroppo the winner
- c) declare it a draw, but say in your report that Aggroppo was dead unlucky

5. At the end of a running race it looks like a dead heat between Nippylon and Whippylon. Who gets the victor's laurel wreath? Do you:
  a) give them half each
  b) award it to the god, Zeus
  c) make them run again

6. The chariot race comes to a spine-tingling finish with ace driver Damonhillon just crossing the line first. Do you award the winner's wreath to:
  a) Damonhillon's horse
  b) Damonhillon
  c) the owner of Damonhillon's horse

7. A runner is guilty of a false start. Do you:
  a) have him flogged
  b) make him go back five paces
  c) disqualify him if he does it again

8. Women aren't allowed in to the Games, but you discover one watching from behind a pillar. Do you:

   a) have her thrown out

   b) have her thrown in jail

   c) have her thrown over the nearest cliff

Answers

1. c) Ugh! The blood came from the animals sacrificed to Zeus and was taken to be holy.

2. a) This is how the saying "starting from scratch" came about.

3. c) Let the fight go on. This is how it was in Pankration. If the other fighter hadn't been dressed the same, then he wouldn't have stood much chance!

4. b) The loser was the one who gave in. Mangulon did, Aggroppo didn't (and never would, of course).

5. b) A pretty good deal for Zeus, who got a victor's wreath without even putting his shorts on.

6. c) All poor old Damonhilion would have got was a piece of ribbon.

7. a) As you can imagine, there weren't too many false starts in the ancient Games.

8. c) What's more, the distance she travelled didn't count for the long jump either!

25

No Ladies, Please!

Competitors who took part in the ancient Games, were easy to spot. They were all:
1. true Greeks
2. not slaves
3. covered in oil
4. stark naked

And, last but not least,
5. men

Women could compete in the Games in only one way, as the owner of a chariot and horses. Even then, women weren't allowed in as spectators. The law was that "any woman discovered at the Olympic Games should be thrown headlong from the mountain of Typaeum" (typped over the edge, in other words!).

Rule number four, of course, made it pretty tricky for a woman to sneak in without being noticed. That's why the rule was introduced, in fact. Because at one Games a woman named Kallipateira *did* sneak in...

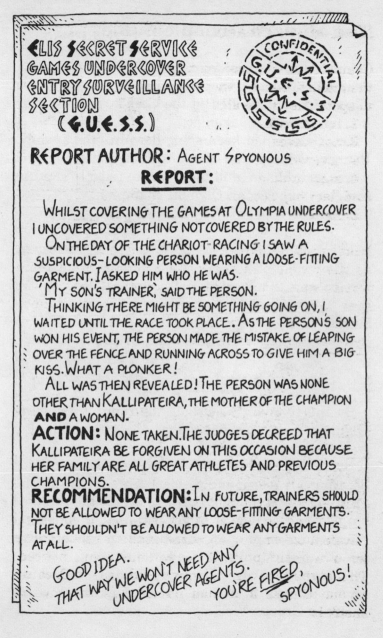

ELIS SECRET SERVICE GAMES UNDERCOVER ENTRY SURVEILLANCE SECTION
(G.U.E.S.S.)

REPORT AUTHOR: Agent Spyonous

REPORT:

Whilst covering the games at Olympia undercover I uncovered something not covered by the rules.

On the day of the chariot-racing I saw a suspicious-looking person wearing a loose-fitting garment. I asked him who he was.

'My son's trainer', said the person.

Thinking there might be something going on, I waited until the race took place. As the person's son won his event, the person made the mistake of leaping over the fence and running across to give him a big kiss. What a plonker!

All was then revealed! The person was none other than Kallipateira, the mother of the champion **AND** a woman.

ACTION: None taken. The judges decreed that Kallipateira be forgiven on this occasion because her family are all great athletes and previous champions.

RECOMMENDATION: In future, trainers should not be allowed to wear any loose-fitting garments. They shouldn't be allowed to wear any garments at all.

GOOD IDEA. THAT WAY WE WON'T NEED ANY UNDERCOVER AGENTS. YOU'RE FIRED, SPYONOUS!

The Modern Olympic Games

The ancient Games were finally abolished in the year AD393 by the Emperor Theodosius. He was a Christian and objected to the Games because they honoured Zeus, a pagan god.

The Games had been going downhill for a while, though. Bribery and cheating had got worse and worse as athletes (and their Kings) tried to capture the glory of being an Olympic champion.

By the time of Theodosius the reputation of the Olympic Games as a festival of honesty and fair play was pretty much gone.

But their memory lingered on. And, as memories do, they got rosier and rosier. People forgot all the grotty bits and thought only about how the athletes trained and struggled to get better at their sports for nothing more than the chance to win an olive wreath to stick on their heads.

Gradually, other "Olympic" Games started up trying to copy what had gone on all those years before in Greece. Well, not copy exactly...

Country Games

One of these Games took place (and still does) in the small village of Wenlock in Shropshire. The Wenlock Olympian Games were started in 1850 by a man named William Penny Brookes. He was a doctor, and wanted to encourage outdoor sports because he thought it was more healthy for the villagers than sitting in a pub all day.

The Wenlock Games had some events that the ancient Greeks would have found very peculiar.

Mind you, the pig chase sounds as though it could have been a pretty dirty event. As a local newspaper report said one year:

'The pig was started in the middle of the field and led its pursuers over hedge and ditch right into town where it took ground in a cellar...'

William Brookes wanted to get the Olympic Games started up again as more than just a small affair. He wanted to see an Olympics in which athletes of different countries competed against each other. His problem was that he couldn't get the support of England's important Amateur Athletic Club. They were an incredibly snooty bunch and most of their athletes came from the upper-classes. They didn't like the idea of competing against grubby working-class people at all!

WORKING CLASS OIK

UPPER CLASS TWIT

But if Brookes didn't manage to convince the Amateur Athletic Club, he did convince one very important man: Baron Pierre de Coubertin, a French aristocrat. De Coubertin believed that playing sport made you a better person. He also thought it was great for bringing people of different countries together – certainly better than the usual way, of fighting a war. When he visited the Wenlock Games, and heard Brookes' idea of reviving the ancient Olympics, he decided to do something about it himself.

The difference between de Coubertin and Brookes was that the Frenchman knew a lot of important people (Aristocrats tend to). In fact he knew so many important people that by 1894, only two years after visiting the Wenlock Games, de Coubertin had managed to set up an International Olympic Committee (IOC).

From there, things moved quickly. This committee met, made arrangements, and generally sorted things out. (Most unusual for a committee!) So much so that, just two years later, on Easter Monday 1896, the first "Olympiad of the Modern Era" began. For obvious reasons it was staged in Athens, Greece.

Over the years, the Games grew in size with more and more countries taking part. More and more sports were introduced, too, including "winter" sports like Ice Hockey

I'M FREEZING

and Figure Skating.

Me too!

In 1924 the summer and winter sports were separated, with the first Winter Olympics being held in Chamonix, France. (The next Winter Games will be held in 1998. Watch out for a book called *Frozen Olympics*!)

And so Pierre de Coubertin's dream has been realised ... or has it? His dream was for the Olympics to be about athletes of all countries meeting in friendly, honest competition – no skulduggery or dirty tricks. Has that been the way? You'll soon find out.

So, start packing! Shorts, running shoes, swimming costume, tennis racket, hockey stick, weightlifting gear, spare horse ... you'll need it all. Oh, yes – and you'd better pack the next chapter in too. It's your crucial guide to what's on...

FLAMING OLYMPIC EVENTS – A DUFFER'S GUIDE

Are you a complete duffer when it comes to sports? Can you tell the difference between a hockey stick and a walking stick? Do you think that badminton is dreadful goodminton, or that weightlifting is carrying your bag home from school?

Then this is the guide for you! Here's the idea behind every Olympic sport, with no confusing complications or jellylegging jargon to put you off.

Amazing Athletics

You do one of three things in athletics: run, jump or throw something.

For a **running** race you go as fast as you can. If it's a short race you go faster, and if it's a long race you go slower. You can still win a short race if you go slower, of course, so long as you go faster than everybody else. In the same way, you can lose a long race by going slower than somebody else who's going slow faster. Get it?

Jumping is either long, high or very high. In long jumping you end up in a sand pit you're not allowed to play in. High jumping is more fun because you dive onto a bouncy castle (without the castle bit), but less fun because there's always a bar in the way! For very high jumping (called pole-vaulting) you get a better bounce, but you have to use a pole which is very awkward to fit into your bag.

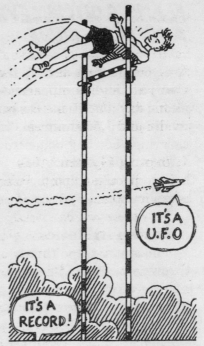

To remember the **throwing** events, think of school dinners. The idea is to throw something as far as you can, and you can choose between a discus (a sort of dinner-less dinner plate), a javelin (a fork with only one prong), a shot (a school-dinner dumpling, but not quite so hard or heavy) or a hammer (a school-dinner dumpling before it's let out of its saucepan).

People who can't make up their mind what they like best can go in for all of them. The **heptathlon** is

34

for women, and involves a mixture of seven events. Men are even worse at making up their mind, so they have a decathlon of ten events, taking place over two days. On the first day, it's the 100 metres, long jump, shot put, high jump and 400 metres, and on the second day it's 110 metres hurdles, discus, pole vault, javelin and 1,500 metres. Phew!

Jumping Gymnastics

A very peculiar sport. Points are scored for doing tricks on strange pieces of equipment, such as:
- a **horse** you can't ride
- a **beam** that doesn't shine
- **rings** that don't make a sound

Gymnasts also do **floor exercises**, in which the idea is to do lots of somersaults – that is, stay off the floor.

You have to be very supple for gymnastics, which is why some people call it gymelastics.

Curious Combat

There are four combat sports.

Fencing is for people with a duel personality. You have a sword which isn't called a sword but either a foil, a saber or an épée. Each of these has a handle end and a pointy end. The pointy end has a button on it so that it isn't too pointy. The idea is to touch the other person with the not-very-pointy end before they touch you. Get the point?

Boxing is like fencing without swords. In boxing you hit the other person with your fists. Boxers come in different weights. The lightest weight is 48kg. This is called light flyweight, even though no 48kg fly has ever been seen. The heaviest weight

is heavyweight. Boxers have always been confused by maths, which is why they fight for three rounds in a square ring and their referee never counts higher than ten!

BUT, MUM!
....

The aim of **wrestling** is to get your opponent to lie down. Mothers are very good at this, especially when fighting children at bedtime, but strangely, women aren't allowed in this event! There are two sorts of wrestling. In "freestyle" you can grab with your arms and legs; in "Greco-Roman" wrestling, you can only use your arms. (So why hasn't an octopus ever been Olympic champion?)

Finally, **Judo**. This is a throwing event (see Athletics), the differences being: a) you throw the other person, and b) it's not how far you throw them that matters, but how often.

THIS WILL BE A SHORT FLING!

Terrific Targets

There are two target sports, **archery** and **shooting**. In both the aim is to aim. It's also to hit as many bull's eyes as possible. In archery you use a bow and arrow. In **shooting** you use a gun and bullet to bull-hit.

The other type of gun shooting is **clay-pigeon** shooting. In this you shoot as many clay pigeons as possible. It's fun, but they taste horrible.

Courting Couples

These are sports played on a court – which is why they usually have a judge nearby. The idea with all of them is to score points by hitting something over a net and out of the reach of your opponent.

In **badminton**, what you hit is a shuttlecock. This is made out of feathers – which is why it flies so well!

Tennis players use a tennis ball. This is made out of rubber and makes a racket when you hit it. Scoring in tennis is very friendly. If you haven't scored any points at all, the judge calls you "love".

A small, light ball is used in **table-tennis**. This sport is played on a table, which is why serving properly is very important. Strangely, a perfect serve is one which the other player can't reach. If you manage this, everybody thinks you're ace.

Tingling Team Sports

It is very easy to get confused between the different team sports, so concentrate hard.

In **football** you hit the ball into the net with your head or your foot; handball is bad.

In **handball** foot-ball is bad; You hit the ball into the net with your hand.

In **volleyball** you don't hit the ball into the net: that's bad. You use your hand to hit the ball *over* the net.

In **basketball** you don't put the ball over the net: that's bad. You don't hit it into the net either: that's bad too. You *throw* the ball into the net.

Hockey is different from all of the others. Foot-ball is bad. Hand-ball is bad. Heading is very very bad. You hit the ball into the net using a wooden thing with a curved end. And if you're not very good at first, what you have to do is stick at it until you get better.

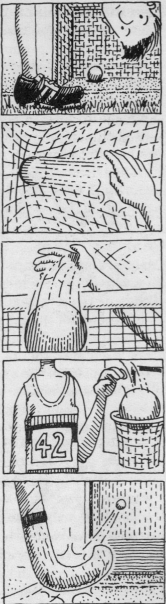

Wonderful Whack-the-Ball Games

There are two of these games and they're very, very similar.

Baseball is all about scoring runs. You have to hit the ball and run round in circles. The side running round in circles the most is the winner. Baseball language can be tricky. When you're batting, the ball is thrown at you by the other side's "pitcher". It's his job to throw it so hard that you can't strike it. If you don't strike it, the umpire shouts "Strike!".

Softball uses a hard ball, but not as hard as a baseball. It's baseball for softies.

Swell Swimming

Swimming is the cleanest of all sports, but the only one you can't learn from the bottom. The idea of all the swimming races is to get out of the water as quickly as possible. Events take place over different distances, and with the swimmers using different "strokes". Funnily enough, the fastest stroke is the crawl.

Diving is dead simple. Watch carefully, and you'll see there are only three parts to it:

1) go up to a high place;

2) jump off and pretend you're doing gymnastics instead;

3) land in the water.

Divers don't have to be swimmers, but it helps. They have to do three dives, and drowning after the first won't score very well. Oh, yes – the diver that makes the biggest splash with the judges is usually the one who makes the smallest splash.

Water polo can only be played at fun times, because you need to have a ball in the pool with you. There are two aims of the game: 1) to throw the ball into the other team's goal, and 2) not to drown. Think of water polo as being a bit like handball with a lot of drips.

Weird Water Events

There are three water events in which the last thing you want to do is go into the water.

Rowing is the only event in the whole of the Olympics in which you can win a gold medal sitting down and facing the wrong way.

Canoeing is the water sport where you don't have a paddle, you use one.

Yachting is the sport in which the equipment costs the most. Boats are very expensive, and certainly can't be bought at the January sails.

Rip-roaring Riding

There are two riding sports in the Olympics and they're both very similar. The first is **cycling**, in which cycles are ridden. The second sport is called **equestrianism**, in which you ride ... yes, an equus. It's the latin word for horse.

Cycles and horses can be tricky to tell apart, because:

- they both have saddles
- neither has brakes
- both leave marks on the road
- both have riders wearing coloured outfits and hard hats.

Top tip: to tell the difference, wait until they stop moving. Horses don't fall over.

Perilous Pentathlon

Last, but not least, for chaps only (sorry, girls!) who really are accident prone, here's the ultimate event:

- **riding** a horse, until it says "neigh, no more!"...
- **fencing** your way out of trouble in a sword duel...
- **shooting** your way out of even more trouble with a pistol...
- **swimming** your way to freedom across a river, before finally...
- **running** 4,000 metres to complete your mission!

It's called the Modern Pentathlon, but the Absolute Murder Pentathlon might be a better description!

OK, that's it! Now you've had a full run-down of the running events, a crash course in the combat events, a deadly accurate guide to the target events and you're one jump ahead about the gymnastics.

So, let's go! First stop the Opening Ceremony. The fun and Games are about to begin!

STRIKE A LIGHT!
THE OPENING CEREMONY

Here we are then. So, what's going to happen?

Well, the ancient Games had an opening ceremony. Remember – when the athletes and judges did a lot of swearing? (Before the events got under way and they did a lot more swearing!)

It's the same with the modern Olympics. In 1896, though, the ceremony was over and done with pretty quickly. There was a procession of all the competitors, the Games were declared open, a bugle sounded and that was it – the first event began.

Nowadays, though, it's not so simple. Over the years more and more bits have been added to the opening ceremony. Come on then, get your official suit on. Let's join the parade at Atlanta in 1996.

The Procession (first happened in 1896)

First into the stadium is the Olympic flag. Then come the different national teams. Hang on, it's not us yet! Greece are always first, because that's where the Olympics began. After them come the teams of the other countries, in alphabetical order. The host country – the United States of America in 1996 – comes last (probably to make sure the crowd stays awake until the end of the procession!).

Olympic Oddity

In 1988 the Olympic games were held in Seoul, South Korea. Greece led in, as usual – but instead of Afghanistan there followed Gabon and Ghana – and there was a good reason for it! What could it have been?

IT'S AS EASY AS G.B.C.!

GROAN!

Boring Speeches (1896)

Here we are at last! That procession took well over an hour! So, what's the last thing you want to have now? A boring speech? Sorry, that's just what you're going to get. Yawn...

Aha! Good news. President Clinton's on his feet. It's his job to declare the Games open, and his speech will be dead short. How can we be sure? It's written for him!

I HEREBY DECLARE OPEN THE TWENTY-SIXTH OLYMPIAD OF THE MODERN ERA IN ATLANTA, GEORGIA.

I WOULD ALSO LIKE TO SAY...

THAT'S ENOUGH!!

The Olympic Oath (1920)

Right, he's back in his seat. Now what? Well, remember in the ancient Games the competitors swore an oath not to cheat or get up to any funny business? That's the next bit. Up you go, you can do it. On behalf of all the athletes you say:

WE SWEAR WE WILL TAKE PART IN THESE OLYMPIC GAMES IN THE TRUE SPIRIT OF SPORTSMANSHIP AND THAT WE WILL RESPECT AND ABIDE BY THE RULES THAT GOVERN THEM FOR THE GLORY OF SPORT AND HONOUR OF OUR COUNTRY.

In other words, "we all promise to play fair". (But it doesn't always happen – as you'll find out in the Champion Cheats chapter!)

The Olympic Flag (1920)

Not going up the pole yet, are you? Good. Because that's the job of the Olympic Flag. There it goes. It's white, with five interlocking rings coloured blue, black, red, yellow and green (because, in 1920, at least one of these colours appeared in the flag of each country taking part in the Games). It's supposed to represent five continents of the world being united in sport.

The Olympic Motto (1924)

The motto contains just three words: *Citius, Altius, Fortius*.

The only problem with it as a motto is that they're Latin words and most people don't know what they mean. (You too, eh? How about your teacher? Oh, dear.)

So, here they are in English: *Swifter, Higher, Stronger*.

Whatever their sport, every Olympic competitor is trying to perform their particular sport to the very best of their ability.

The Olympic Flame (1928)

OK, the ceremony's hotting up a bit now. We're getting ready to light the Olympic Flame. It'll stay alight all the while the Games are on. Now, where's that flaming torch...

The Torch Relay (1936)

Ah, here it comes. It's being carried by the last runner in a relay that's brought it all the way from Olympia. The idea of the torch relay comes from the ancient Games. In those days there was a fun event called the *lampadedromia* – a torch race. It was a relay with six to ten teams, except that instead of a baton, runners had to carry a lighted torch! The winners were the first team home with the torch still alight, and to them went the honour of lighting the sacred flame.

Fancy organising the relay another year? Right, here's what you'll have to do:

MOST IMPORTANT: DO NOT LET THE TORCH GO OUT! EVEN MORE IMPORTANT: IF IT DOES GO OUT AND YOU HAVE TO LIGHT IT AGAIN, MAKE SURE NOBODY SEES YOU!

The first relay in 1936 covered 3,000km, with the torch being carried by runners doing 1km each. This is still the way it's done, although sometimes part of the journey is made by sea or air.

WHY DIDN'T YOU GET THE BOAT?

(Or laser beam! For the Montreal Olympics in 1976 the flame's energy was used to send a laser beam from Greece which ended up by lighting an identical torch in Canada.)

At the end of the relay the final runner enters the stadium and trots round the track (trying desperately not to cough or sneeze), climbs a flight of steps and lights the Olympic flame in a large cereal bowl filled with stuff that's guaranteed to snap, crackle and pop for the whole time the Games are on.

In Barcelona in 1992 they tried something different. The runner used the Olympic torch to light an archer's arrow ... slowly, the archer took aim at the big bowl, high up on the far side of the stadium ... he drew back the bowstring ... fired ... the flaming arrow shot off into the night sky ... and the Olympic flame burst into life!

HE'S A HOT SHOT!

It looked like the archer had been incredibly accurate, but in fact he could have missed by a mile. Things had been rigged so that the flame would light up anyway.

It's For You-Hoo!

How about this for a different kind of Olympic ring? The opening procession had ended and all the competitors were gathered in the middle of the arena. Everybody was waiting intently for the next part of the ceremony when suddenly – a telephone rang! It was a call for the USA athlete, Carl Lewis, who still had his portable phone in his blazer pocket.

Phew! That's the opening ceremonies over. All very nice, but now it's time to get on with the real stuff. Three weeks of running and jumping and swimming and cycling and generally going round the bend.

So, better have a quick look round while you've got a chance. Where's everything happening? And who are you going to be up against...

HOT HOLIDAYS AND COLD WARS: THE COMPETITORS

It took the host city a whole year to prepare for the ancient Games. Sorting out the stadium and getting ready for the crowds of competitors, judges and spectators was a major task. (Pity they didn't have a Heracles around to help!)

Nowadays, though, even a year wouldn't be anything like long enough. The host city is chosen *six* years in advance! Atlanta, hosts to the 100th anniversary Games in 1996, were chosen in September 1990.

Why so long? Because there's usually a lot of building to do and a lot of arrangements to make. Every sport in the Games needs its own stadium or playing area, for a start. Then there are the people who will be coming, from over 170 different countries.

The Numbers Game

Try these numbers questions about the 1996 Games...

1. About how many competitors are expected in Atlanta?

2. And how many officials?

3. How many spectators are expected to turn up to watch?

4. How many people are expected to watch the Games on television?

Add to all these the hundreds of newspaper reporters ... the TV and film crews ... the hot-dog sellers ... and it all adds up to a lot of people needing somewhere to stay and something to eat.

The athletes come first, of course. A special "village" is built for them to live in. Although sometimes "village" is too grand a word...

Five Things you Didn't Know About Olympic Villages

1. In the ancient Games they didn't have one! The athletes had to find somewhere to live themselves. Even worse, all those sweaty runners, wrestlers, boxers, pankrationists and charioteers had to share just two bath houses! It's a wonder they weren't called the Oh-stinky Games.

2. The 1920 Games were held in Antwerp, in Belgium. The "village" was actually a school building.

3. Los Angeles in 1932 saw the first purpose-built village – for men only! To make sure that women athletes (women of any description, in fact) didn't get in, the village was guarded by cowboys. The women athletes – all 127 of them – shared a hotel.

4. The 1948 Games in London were the first to take place after World War II, and there wasn't the money or the materials to spend on special housing for athletes. So they were put in Army camps.

(The men lost out this time – the women stayed in much nicer college accommodation.)

5. In 1952, two Olympic villages were built. One for the men and one for the women, you think? No – one for the communist countries (who were suspicious of everybody else) and one for everybody else.

The Olympic village in Atlanta will be much grander. Not only will it have rooms for the athletes to live in, but come complete with a shopping mall, discos, bowling alley and a cinema!

DiscO-lympian!

At the 1992 Games, the computer system containing results flashed up the message:

54

Countries Taking Part

More and more competitors and countries have joined the Olympics since they were started again in 1896. Then there were just 311 competitors – and 230 of those were from Greece, where the Games were taking place!

In fact, for the first few Olympiads, most of the athletes did come from the host country. Why? Because of the time taken to travel from overseas. In those days, the fastest way of travelling was by boat. And there were other problems – as the team from America found out...

MRS IDA HO,
IDAHO,
U.S.A.

Athens, Greece

15TH April, 1896

Dear Mom,

Are we having an amazing time! I've sure got a lot of news to report from here in little ol' Greece. Some of it's been bad and some of it's been good - so here goes, BAD NEWS: The boat trip from America took 17 days. Not what you'd call plain sailing!

GOOD NEWS: When we finally got here, though, the Greek people were real pleased to see us. They threw a party for us and kept us up all night eating and drinking. Especially drinking.

BAD NEWS: Next morning we found out that we'd got our dates wrong. The Greeks run a different calendar to us and the start of the Games wasn't a week away like we thought. They were due to start that day! And for some reason I had a real bad headache, Mommie....

GOOD NEWS: Even so, we won 11 gold medals between us. Maybe we should go drinking every night! (Only Joking Mom! I stuck to milk shakes all the time.)

Your loving son and Olympic
athlete,
Hank

Over the years travel has become a bit easier! With the Olympic Games growing in popularity, more and more countries have sent teams to compete. In Barcelona in 1992 no less than 172 countries were represented, the biggest number ever.

Guns or Games

Baron de Coubertin's idea that the Games should take the place of wars hasn't always managed to get through to the Generals, though. In ancient times, wars would be held up while the Olympics were on. Every king would sign a "peace treaty" saying something like:

I, KING OF WHATSIT, DO HEREBY AGREE THAT FOR THE DURATION OF THE SACRED OLYMPIAD, WE WHATSITS WILL NOT TAKE UP ARMS, PURSUE LEGAL DISPUTES, OR ANYTHING ELSE LIKELY TO ENDANGER ATHLETES AND SPECTATORS HEADING FOR OLYMPIA. AND IF WE BREAK THIS AGREEMENT, THEN WE WHATSITS WILL PAY A FINE OF ONE TALENT OF SILVER TO ZEUS AT OLYMPIA.

In modern times it hasn't worked this way. The Games have been cancelled instead. This has happened three times.

- In 1916, the 6th Olympiad was given the bullet because World War I got in the way.
- In 1940 and 1944, the 12th and 13th Olympiads were bombed out because World War II was being fought.

Did you know? Olympiad numbers count, even if the Games don't take place. So the Centenary Games in Atlanta will still be called the 26th Olympiad, even though they'll only be the 23rd Games to have been held.

I'm not playing with you, so there!

Even though the Olympics have been held at all other times, not everybody has been there! In fact only Australia, France, Greece, Great Britain and Switzerland have been at every Games since 1896. How come? Well, athletes swear an oath that sport will come first – but the politicians don't. And what a mess that makes...

- In 1920 Germany, Austria, Hungary and Turkey (the countries on the losing side in World War I) weren't invited.
- By 1924 Germany still hadn't been forgiven; they weren't invited back until the next Games in 1928.
- In 1948, Germany and Japan (the countries on the losing side in World War II) weren't invited. Russia and the other communist countries were invited but decided to stay away.
- From 1964 to 1992 South Africa weren't invited because of their policy of apartheid (treating people differently depending on the colour of their skin).

58

- In 1980 the Olympics were held in Russia. As they'd just invaded Afghanistan, the United States, West Germany and Japan stayed away as a protest.
- In 1984, the Games were held in the United States – so Russia stayed at home to pay America back for 1980!

Money, money, money

For many years (until 1992) the other restriction was that you weren't allowed in to the Olympics if you were a professional – that is, if you earned money from playing sport. Baron de Coubertin insisted on this. His view was that a professional's only aim is to win the prize money and that they couldn't care tuppence for simply taking part (but if they had cared tuppence that would have made them professionals, wouldn't it? Hmm...).

For a long time, the Baron's successors said the same, although nobody really believed that every athlete taking part didn't really earn money from their sports. But, so long as they weren't found out, it was all right...

The Greatest Athlete in The World

Jim Thorpe of America won both the Pentathlon and Decathlon in the 1912 Games (a total of 15 events!) by wide margins. When presenting him with his medals, King Gustav of Sweden told Thorpe "Sir, you are the greatest athlete in the world!"

But a year later it was revealed that Thorpe had once accepted a small amount of money for coaching American football players in the holidays – which made him a professional. Even though the people he beat in the 1912 Games refused to accept his medals, Thorpe still had them taken away and his name was removed from the Olympic records.

It wasn't until 1982 – 70 years later, and nearly 30 years after Thorpe's death in 1953 – that this unfair decision was reversed and his medals given back to his family.

'Ere we go ... Competitors & Teams

Until 1912, there were no official teams. Competitors entered as individuals, or as groups of friends who fancied the outing – anybody who turned up could enter! Like the Irishman, John Boland, who just happened to be on holiday...

John Boland won the tennis singles! He also teamed up with a German partner and won the doubles. An ace performer!

Another winner was an Australian, Edwin Flack, who'd been working in London when he heard about the Olympics. He promptly took a month's holiday and toddled off to Greece to take part. When he came back he had something really different to show around the office – winning medals for the 800 and 1,500 metres races.

Some countries did send teams to Greece, but they weren't official. The Americans, for instance, were all college students and had arranged to go together.

As for the British team – well, most of the best athletes didn't go. Why? Because the best were all incredibly snooty Oxford and Cambridge University students – and they were objecting because the invitation to take part in the Games had been written in French!

Trials and Tribulations!

Nowadays, countries send official teams, and most of them hold trials to choose the people who will go to the Olympics.

One US runner had a particularly tough time winning his place. Boyd Gittens was taking part in the trial for the 100 metre hurdles race in the 1972 Olympics in Mexico. This is what happened...

1. He got to his marks.
2. He got set.
3. When the starter's gun went off, he flew down the track.
4. The trouble was, a pigeon flew down the track too. And, unlike Boyd, the pigeon hadn't been to the toilet before the race. So...
5. The pigeon let rip there and then. And, as we all know, droppings drop...

6. Which this one did – right in Boyd Gitten's eye...

7. Knocking out his contact lens! He couldn't go on and – you've guessed it – he had to "drop" out of the race!

There was almost a happy ending, though. They ran the trial again. This time, Boyd qualified for the team and went to Mexico – where this happened...

1. He didn't get to his marks.

2. He didn't get set.

He'd got an injured leg and couldn't run!

Oly The Slowly

Not all teams are picked in the same way, though. In 1976, Olemus Charles from Haiti ran the worst ever time for the 10km race. He took over 42 minutes (the usual time is about 28 mins) and by the time he finished, everybody else was getting changed. It was then discovered that Olemus wasn't really a runner at all, and he'd never competed in a big event. Haiti hadn't held any trials at all. The dictator of the country had given out places in the Olympics as rewards. Oly the Slowly had won his trip through being a good office worker!

63

Olympic Names

Maybe it would be better if countries just picked their teams by looking at names. Here are some names of gold-medal winners:

● Robert **WEAVER** (USA) weaved his way to a wrestling gold medal in 1984.

● Joaquim **CRUZ** (BRA) positively cruzed to the winning line in the 1984 800m.

● Duncan **ARMSTRONG** (AUS) must have found strong arms helpful in winning the 200m free-style swimming in 1988.

● James **LIGHTBODY** (USA) probably had one after winning the 800m, 1,500m and 2,500m steeplechase events in 1904.

● and Frank **SHORTER** (USA) probably was after pounding over 26 miles of road to win the 1972 marathon.

● Walter **BATHE** (GER) was obviously at home in a pool. In 1912 he sank the opposition to win the 400m backstroke race.

● Edward **FERRY** (USA) ferried himself beautifully to win a gold for rowing in 1964.

But it doesn't always work. For instance,

● Reg **WALKER** (SAF) certainly didn't. He won the 100m sprint in 1908.

● The Swedish runner Ens **FAST** was badly named too. He got lost in the 1900 marathon!

And how about **PAPADIAMANTOP PAPADIAMANTOPOULOS**! What do you think a man with a name like that could do?

Answer: What's the only job possible for a man with a never-ending name? Starter, of course! He fired the gun at the 1896 Games.

Ladies AND Gentlemen!

As we saw earlier, women weren't allowed to enter the ancient Games. Well, when Baron de Coubertin started the modern Olympics his view was that exactly the same number should enter the modern Olympics! He said:

He got his way in 1896 – not a single woman was allowed to take part! In 1900 things improved slightly (they could hardly get any worse) with 12 women taking part. Only two events were open to them: tennis and golf!

Over the years, though, more and more women have taken part in the Games. In 1992 over 2000 women competed – a much higher number, but still nothing like as many as the over 8000 men.

The number of events has grown too. Now there are women's sections in most sports. Which of these ten sports won't have women competitors in 1996?

1. Archery	6. Hockey
2. Canoeing	7. Judo
3. Cycling	8. Shooting
4. Equestrian	9. Volleyball
5. Football	10. Wrestling

Answer: Only one – wrestling. The other events in which women don't compete – yet – are boxing, modern pentathlon and weightlifting. A women's football tournament will be held for the first time in 1996. In the equestrian, shooting and yachting events, women compete against men.

How rude!

It's been a long struggle for acceptance, though. Lots of nasty things have been said, and women have had to prove people wrong. Here are some of the times it's happened!

- In 1928, women competed in athletics events for the first time: the 100m, 800m, 4x100m relay, discus and high jump. After the 800m, Baron de Coubertin complained that the tired women provided "a very unedifying spectacle for the spectators". After this, women weren't allowed to run more than 200m until 1964. They now have their own marathon.

- A woman is the only athlete to have won medals at running, jumping and throwing events. In 1932, Mildred "Babe" Didrikson (USA) won the 80m hurdles and javelin gold medals, and got silver in the high jump.

● When the 31-year-old Dutch woman athlete Francina "Fanny" Blankers-Koen turned up at the London Olympics in 1948, the British team manager, Jack Crump, said she was "too old to win anything". She promptly won four gold medals in the 100m, 200m, 80m hurdles and 4x100m relay – and Jack crumpled!

But of all the brilliant women athletes there have been at the Olympics, perhaps the two most unlikely were these...

The Two Sickly Kids

Dawn Fraser was born on 4 September 1937. She was the youngest of eight children, four boys and four girls, living in an old semi-detached house.

The house was in a run-down area, not far from where the ships lay at anchor in Sydney docks. It was as if Dawn Fraser was meant to be close to water.

She was spoilt pretty rotten as a baby. All those brothers and sisters to cuddle her! "Dawnie, Dawnie," they'd sing into her ear, and she'd gurgle merrily.

It wasn't long, though, before the gurgling turned to coughing. As she grew up it seemed that if there was a cold going, Dawn would catch it. The trouble was, it wouldn't just give her a runny nose, then go away. It would hang around, spreading to her lungs

68

and ending up in a bout of asthma. When this happened it was scarey for everybody.

"I can't breathe!" she'd gasp. "It feels like I've got a kangaroo sitting on my chest!" (This might sound funny, but it wasn't. Kangaroos are as heavy as a small car.) Sometimes the asthma was so bad Dawn would have to sleep sitting up in bed, afraid to lay down in case it made her start coughing again.

And then, one day in 1943, when Dawn was six years old, her brother Don took her to the swimming pool. As she splashed around in the water, breathing in the warm, moist air, Dawn felt something happening to her. Her lungs felt better. She didn't feel like coughing so much.

Maybe if she learnt to swim it would help her even more...

Thousands of miles away, in the Southern state of Tennessee in the United States of America, another little girl was having troubles with her health. Her name was Wilma Rudolph. She was three years younger than Dawn Fraser, but also from a big family. Dawn might have thought her family of eight was big, but if she'd had the chance Wilma would have told Dawn she didn't know what "big" meant – Wilma was the youngest of twelve children!

Wilma's family suffered by being picked on because they were black. They were also very poor, and often hungry. Like Dawn Fraser though, the only thing Wilma didn't miss out on was illness. As the years went by, Wilma caught scarlet fever, double pneumonia (a disease in both lungs) and then, at the age of six, the worst of the lot – polio. It left her with a paralysed right leg.

"Good job there's a lot of us, Wilma," her brothers and sisters would say, "we can take it in turns to rub it back to life for you!"

And rub her leg they did, four times a day, every day. Wilma did her bit too. She was absolutely determined to walk like everybody else. But she had to be patient. She still needed a metal brace on her leg when she was eight, and couldn't walk far without having somebody to help her.

She kept working and exercising. It took her a further four years to make her leg strong enough to stand on her own. She was able to swap the leg brace for a special shoe – but still she wasn't satisfied. Now she wanted to run properly.

Her brothers played basketball. With so many of

them, they almost had their own team! Wilma began to join in, hopping around in her special shoe. She played and played, exercised and exercised, until one day the shoe felt just too heavy. Wilma took it off. It was the day she'd dreamt of. In her bare feet, the twelve-year-old Wilma Rudolph started running...

Dawn Fraser was fifteen by then, and still swimming. After that first time in the public swimming pool, she'd gone as often as she could (usually getting in for free by jumping over the turnstile in the middle of a gang of boys). Her brother Don had taught her to swim, sometimes by diving from the high board with Dawn on his back!

She'd joined a swimming club, and won her first race – against grown women! By the time she was twelve she was winning races regularly, and looking forward to the day when she could pick up the small cash prizes her swimming club gave to winners who were over sixteen.

And then – she was banned! After winning a championship race, Dawn Fraser was accused of being a professional! The reason? Because of the money prizes the club gave. In spite of the fact that Dawn wasn't sixteen, hadn't won any money, and didn't even belong to the club any more, she wasn't allowed to enter competitions for eighteen months. But she kept on training, riding her bike twenty miles a day to get to swimming lessons.

Dawn Fraser wanted an Olympic gold medal...

By then, so did Wilma Rudolph. Once she'd started running, she couldn't stop. Her legs, a pain for so long, were now her greatest joy. They were growing, long and graceful. Her speed was improving, day by day. She was getting faster, racing over 100 metres and 200 metres in quicker and quicker times.

By the age of fifteen, the painful days of limping and being helped around were far behind her. She was now winning American sprint championships. Asked about this miracle, Wilma would just joke about the size of her family. "I had to learn to run fast," she'd say, "otherwise there was nothing left to eat by the time I got to the table!"

Just one year later, Wilma Rudolph found herself sitting on an aeroplane. The girl who couldn't walk properly only a few years before was on her way to compete in the 1956 Olympic Games – in Melbourne,

Australia, the home of Dawn Fraser. Dawn was competing, too.

The two sickly girls had made it to the top of the class.

That year, Dawn Fraser won the 100m free-style swimming gold medal in a world-record time. Four years later, in 1960, Dawn won the 100m free-style again, the first woman to win this race two Games in succession.

In 1956, at just 16 years of age, Wilma Rudolph won a bronze medal as a member of the American 4x100m relay team. Her time was to come. In 1960, Wilma Rudolph was the talk of the Olympics as she won the 100m and 200m sprints and ran a stunning last leg to help her country to victory in the 4x100m relay.

ABSOLUTE TORCH-URE: FLAMING OLYMPICS TRAINING

To be an Olympic champion needs dedication. That runner or swimmer or cyclist or boxer or gymnast has probably given up everything to train for their running, swimming, cycling, boxing or ... er, gymnasticalling.

So, do flaming Olympians enjoy training, or do they find it absolute torch-ure? Well, training to be a champion has always been tough...

How did competitors train for the ancient Games?

1. Competitors used to rub linseed oil into their skin.   TRUE/FALSE

2. Everybody started training ten months before the Games.   TRUE/FALSE

3. If you weren't fit enough the day before the Games started, you wouldn't be allowed to compete.   TRUE/FALSE

4. Boxers strengthened their muscles by breaking up the ground with a pick.   TRUE/FALSE

5. Discus and javelin throwers trained by listening to pop music.   TRUE/FALSE

6. Runners warmed up by beating their vests.   TRUE/FALSE

7. Shortly before the Games started,
competitors went on a strict diet
of bread and milk. TRUE/FALSE

Flaming Food Fads

As we're always being told, eating the right things makes you healthy. (And eating the wrong things makes you happy!) For an athlete, of course, eating the right sort of food is an important part of getting into peak condition. So, if you want to be a champ you've got to chomp the right stuff!

Here are some of the foods Olympic champions have eaten. Not all of them were terribly healthy –

but they worked! Why not check other people's trolleys the next time you're at a supermarket? You might spot an Olympian in training!

• Dried figs

They certainly made Charmis the Spartan run! He trained on dried figs before winning the two-stade footrace in 668BC.

• French wine

The French runners in the 1932 Olympics in Los Angeles claimed wine was an essential part of their diet. Although alcohol was banned in the USA at that time, their wine was allowed.

• Chewing gum

Eddie Tolan, 200m winner in 1932, liked to get stuck into his gum while he set about chewing up the other runners.

• Beer

Bevil Rudd (SAF) used to delight in lazing around with a glass of beer in his hand while he watched other athletes training hard.

• Raw carrots, raw onions, raw spinach, raw cabbage, raw most things

Herb Elliott, the Australian 1,500m champion in 1960, had a diet of natural foods which he always ate raw.

- **5 yoghurts, 10 pieces of fruit, 4 cups of tea, 2 coffees, 2 pastries, large amounts of meat, fish, milk and cheese – and as much parsley as possible**

This was what Mahmoud Gammoudi of Tunisia (who won the 5,000m in 1968) used to eat – every day!

- **Sherry and raw eggs (but they must be mixed together!)**

The USA athletes Murchison, Scholz, Paddock and Kirksey (all 100m finalists in 1920) used to drink this mixture. Ugh!

And, finally,

- **One ox (freshly-sacrificed)**

Milo of Croton was the strongman superstar of the ancient Games, winning the wrestling title in six successive Olympiads. He was so strong that it's said he once lifted a four-year-old ox that had just been sacrificed and carried it round the stadium on his shoulders. What was the secret of his great strength? Well, he was no vegetarian. When he put the ox down he ate it – in a day!

Add Some Zest To Your Training

There's no substitute for hard work, though. If you want to be an Olympic champion you've got grit your teeth (or take them out) and get on with it. But it can be boring, so it's a good idea to do something just that little bit different now and again to liven things up. Which dodges livened up training for these three champion athletes?

1. Emil Zatopeck of Czechoslovakia won the 10,000m in 1948. In 1952, he won the 5,000m, 10,000m and the marathon! In training, did he:
  a) run with a sack of potatoes on his back
  b) run with a lump of concrete on his back
  c) run with Mrs Zatopeck on his back

2. Paavo Nurmi of Finland won the 10,000m track and 10,000m cross-country in 1920. Four years later he won the 10,000m cross-country again, together with the 1,500m and 5,000m on the track. All told, he won nine Olympic medals. In training, did he:
  a) race against mail trains
  b) race against cars
  c) race against the family dog

3. Harold Abrahams of Great Britain won the 100m in 1924. His coach, Sam Mussabini, would make him:

a) do the splits
b) pick up pieces of paper
c) ballet dance

Answers:

1. c) – and Zatopeck's wife, Dana, was no shrimp, either. She won the women's javelin in the 1952 Olympics! In training Zatopeck would also get up at 6am every day (leaving his wife in bed) and run 10 to 25 miles wearing his army boots. That way his legs felt stronger when he had his running spikes on.

2. a) Nurmi would also do short sprints when he finished work, go for a run in the forest before dinner and then end the day by jumping and throwing his arms about.

3. b) – but he had to do it with his running spikes! To help make sure Harold was stretching his legs far enough, the pieces of paper were placed exactly where Mussabini thought Abrahams' feet should land during a race.

It Ain't Half Hot Mum!

Sometimes there's extra training that athletes have to go in for – it's called acclimatisation. If the Games are being held in a cold country, for instance, and you come from a hot one, then you need to do some training in cold temperatures to get used to what it's like. On the other hand, if the Games are being held in a city high above sea-level (where the air is thinner, making it harder to breathe), then you need to do some training at that height.

Pretend you're the 50km walker, Don Thompson, in 1960. It's going to be hot and humid in Rome, and you come from chilly Britain. This is how to acclimatise.

It worked for Don Thompson. He won the gold medal.

The right gear

Wearing the right clothing can also be important. That was certainly so in one event at the ancient Games. This was the "running in armour" race, in which every competitor had to dress head to toe in the armour of a Greek soldier.

Well – it was head to toe until the day this happened...

SPRINTING SENSATION!

ORSIPPES TRIPS UP!!

THE 'RUNNING-IN-ARMOUR' RACE ENDED IN A SENSATION AT YESTERDAY'S OLYMPIC GAMES IN ELIS WHEN HOT FAVOURITE ORSIPPES OF MEGARA LOST HIS TITLE AND A LOT MORE BESIDES!

AT THE STARTING LINE, THOUGH THERE'D BEEN NO HINT OF WHAT WAS TO COME. ORSIPPES LOOKED SPLENDID IN HIS FULL OUTFIT. HIS HELMET SHONE. HIS CHEST PLATE SHONE. HIS LEG PLATES SHONE HIS SHORTS DIDN'T SHINE THEY SHIMMERED. AND AS FOR HIS SHIELD..., NEVER HAS A SOLDIER'S SHIELD SHIMMERED AND SHONE LIKE THAT SOLDIER'S SHIELD.

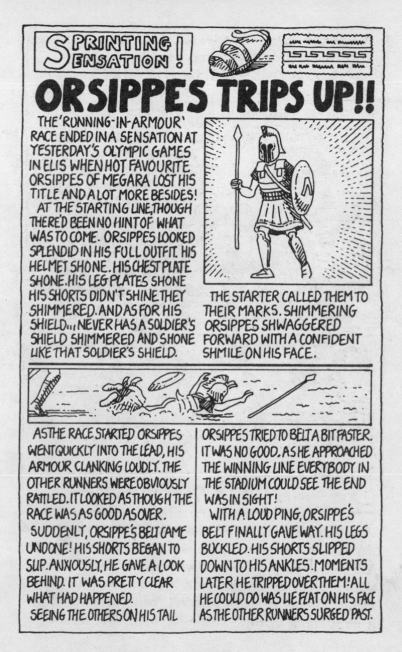

THE STARTER CALLED THEM TO THEIR MARKS. SHIMMERING ORSIPPES SHWAGGERED FORWARD WITH A CONFIDENT SHMILE ON HIS FACE.

AS THE RACE STARTED ORSIPPES WENT QUICKLY INTO THE LEAD, HIS ARMOUR CLANKING LOUDLY. THE OTHER RUNNERS WERE OBVIOUSLY RATTLED. IT LOOKED AS THOUGH THE RACE WAS AS GOOD AS OVER.

SUDDENLY, ORSIPPE'S BELT CAME UNDONE! HIS SHORTS BEGAN TO SLIP. ANXIOUSLY, HE GAVE A LOOK BEHIND. IT WAS PRETTY CLEAR WHAT HAD HAPPENED.

SEEING THE OTHERS ON HIS TAIL

ORSIPPES TRIED TO BELT A BIT FASTER. IT WAS NO GOOD. AS HE APPROACHED THE WINNING LINE EVERYBODY IN THE STADIUM COULD SEE THE END WAS IN SIGHT!

WITH A LOUD PING, ORSIPPE'S BELT FINALLY GAVE WAY. HIS LEGS BUCKLED. HIS SHORTS SLIPPED DOWN TO HIS ANKLES. MOMENTS LATER HE TRIPPED OVER THEM! ALL HE COULD DO WAS LIE FLAT ON HIS FACE AS THE OTHER RUNNERS SURGED PAST.

'THEY ALL LAUGHED AT ME' SAID ORSIPPES AFTER THE RACE. 'WHAT A CHEEK!'

HE SOUNDED VERY SORE ABOUT THINGS—NOT TOO SURPRISING CONSIDERING THE RESULT HAD LEFT HIM IN BOTTOM POSITION!

THE SAME THING WILL NEVER HAPPEN AGAIN, THOUGH. FROM NOW ON, COMPETITORS WILL WEAR ONLY A HELMET AND CARRY A SHIELD. THEY WILL **NOT** WEAR SHORTS AT ALL.

AS ONE OFFICIAL TOLD ME: 'NEXT TIME, WHEN THE RACE STARTS AND THE CROWD SHOUT 'THEY'RE OFF!' IT'LL MEAN JUST THAT.'

THE NEW LOOK

This actually happened to a runner once during the "running-in-armour" race at the ancient Games. After that they did away with shorts and the rest, the runners only wearing a helmet and carrying a shield. Obviously they couldn't "bear" the thought of it happening again!

Did You Know...

about these athletes who also insisted on wearing the right gear?

● **Livio Berruti** of Italy always ran with sunglasses on – presumably to put the other runners in the shade!

● **Herb Elliott** of Australia wore running shoes made out of kangaroo-hide. They put him one jump ahead!

● But neither **Zola Budd** of South Africa nor **Abebe Bikila** of Ethiopia wore shoes at all. They hoped they'd show the others a clean pair of heels!

All a bit different from one runner, who did quite the opposite in 1896 and wore something he never usually wore. Realising that King George I of Greece would be watching, a French sprinter put on a pair of gloves out of politeness because he was running in front of royalty. He didn't win a medal, but when it came to style – you had to hand it to him!

So, you've trained and trained, you've eaten all the right food and you're wearing all the right gear – now comes the big question. What event are you going in for?

SCORCHING PERFORMANCES–SUPERSTARS AND SIZZLING SPECTATORS

The Olympic Games are a bit like a school timetable. New subjects come in, and others go out (usually the ones you like!). Deciding which sports are in or out of the Olympics is the job of the International Olympic Committee – or IOC for short. They try to be fair to everybody. Unlike the Emperor Nero when he took over the ancient Games...

RIGHT, I WANT SOME NEW EVENTS IN THIS YEAR'S GAMES!

ER... WHAT SORT OF EVENTS EMPEROR?

THINGS I'M BRILLIANT AT, OF COURSE! LIKE SINGING. AND ACTING AND I WANT A TEN-HORSE CHARIOT RACE, AS WELL.

BUT NOBODY ELSE HAS A TEN-HORSE CHARIOT.

This scandal took place in AD67 and – surprise, surprise! – Nero won all the events he went in for. He even won the chariot race after being thrown out of his ten-horse chariot and not finishing the race! His name isn't in the record book any more though. When the nutty Emperor was persuaded to commit suicide a year later, the Games were declared invalid and the judges made to pay the money back.

Medals, medals, medals

Events in the modern Olympics have changed quite a lot. We saw in Chapter Two the different sports that will be played in the 1996 Centenary Games. Here's the complete list, with the total number of gold medals up for grabs. Which sports do you think were in the first modern Games 100 years ago?

SPORT	MEDALS TO BE WON
ARCHERY	4
ATHLETICS	44, DIVIDED BETWEEN TRACK AND FIELD EVENTS
BADMINTON	5
BASEBALL	1 TEAM MEDAL
BASKETBALL	2
BOXING	11, 1 FOR EACH WEIGHT DIVISION. MEN ONLY.
CANOE / KAYAK	16
CYCLING	14, 2 MOUNTAIN BIKE, 4 ROAD + 8 TRACK RACING
EQUESTRIAN	6, DIVIDED BETWEEN INDIVIDUAL AND TEAM EVENTS.
FENCING	10

SPORT	MEDALS TO BE WON
FOOTBALL	2 TEAM - 1 MEN, 1 WOMEN
HANDBALL	2 TEAM - 1 MEN, 1 WOMEN
HOCKEY	2 TEAM - 1 MEN, 1 WOMEN
JUDO	14
MOD. PENTATHLON	1 MEDAL, MEN ONLY.
ROWING	14
SHOOTING	15
SOFTBALL	1 MEDAL, WOMEN ONLY.
TABLE TENNIS	4, SINGLES AND DOUBLES
TENNIS	4, SINGLES AND DOUBLES
VOLLEYBALL	4, 2 FOR BEACH VOLLEYBALL + 2 FOR INDOOR
WEIGHTLIFTING	10, MEN ONLY.
WRESTLING	20, MEN ONLY.
YACHTING	10

Extinct Events

Quite a few sports have been in the Olympics – and then out again. Here are some flaming facts about some of them:

Obstacle Race

This was a 200 metres race. Here's what you had to do between the start and finish lines:

- climb over a pole
- scramble over a row of upturned boats
- scramble *under* a row of upturned boats

Not easy, eh? Oh yes, one other thing. The track the race was run on was:

- the River Seine

Yes, it was a swimming race! It only appeared in the Paris games of 1900, then went down the plug-hole.

Rugby

Rugby was discontinued after the 1924 Olympics in Paris. A pity really, it sounded fun – particularly the game in which USA beat the home team, France. After two of the French players were injured, Nelson of the USA was knocked unconscious – by a walking stick wielded by one of the spectators!

Everybody joined in the fight then, and at the end of the match the USA team had to be escorted from the pitch by the police. Could be that's why rugby was booted into touch as an Olympic sport.

Standing long jump

Until 1908, there were standing high and long jump events. The idea was that you jumped from where you were, rather than taking a run-up. The absolute star at this was the American Ray Ewry, who won a total of eight gold medals. His success was all down to his doctor. Ewry suffered from rheumatic fever and the doctor's prescription told him to take up running and jumping to get his strength back.

Try the Standing Long Jump! Here's How:

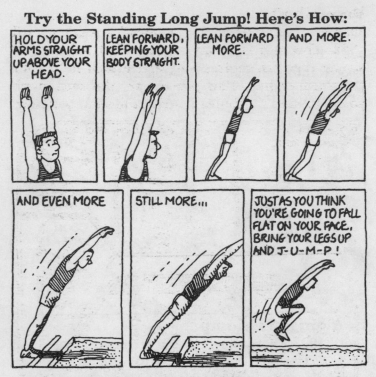

HOLD YOUR ARMS STRAIGHT UP ABOVE YOUR HEAD.

LEAN FORWARD, KEEPING YOUR BODY STRAIGHT.

LEAN FORWARD MORE.

AND MORE.

AND EVEN MORE

STILL MORE....

JUST AS YOU THINK YOU'RE GOING TO FALL FLAT ON YOUR FACE, BRING YOUR LEGS UP AND J-U-M-P!

YOU'VE ALREADY FALLEN FLAT ON YOUR FACE? TOUGH. GO BACK TO STEP 1. WHEN YOU CAN JUMP 3·33 METRES YOU'LL BE AS GOOD AS RAY EWRY.

Tug-of-War

This was discontinued in 1920. It had its moments, though.

In 1908, the Liverpool Police were representing Great Britain and they beat a USA team in seconds. The Americans lodged a protest, saying that the policemen had special boots with spikes, steel cleats and heels. The police argued, saying the boots weren't special at all. They were the boots they wore every day on the beat!

Rope Climb

This was an event in the gymnastics section until 1932. The idea is pretty simple. Find a length of strong rope ten metres long and attach it to your classroom ceiling. Now you can try the rope climb yourself. Here's a simple flowchart to show you how:

Raymond Bass of the USA was the last winner of a rope climbing gold medal. He did the ten metres in 6.7 seconds!

Olympic Ode-ity!

Great Britain won a gold medal in 1896 for an event that didn't exist – and never has! A scholar, Sir George Robertson read an ode (a poem) praising the Greek King. The king was so delighted he awarded Robertson an honorary medal!

The Mind-boggling marathon

The Marathon is probably the most famous event in the whole of the Olympic games. It's a running race which commemorates the run a Greek messenger called Pheidippides is supposed to have made in 490BC. In those days they didn't have postboxes or postvans. So, if somebody wanted to send a letter, they:

1. wrote it
2. stuck it in an envelope
3. put an address on the front
4. gave the envelope to somebody like Pheidippedes
5. said, "Get going, Pheidippedes. You're supposed to be a first-class male!"

This is just what happened on the day in question. The Greeks had defeated the Persians in a battle on the Plain of Marathon and Pheidippedes' boss, Miltiades, wanted everybody in their home city of Athens to know about his triumph as soon as possible.

The trouble was, Athens was a bit far off – like, 280km kind of far off. Still, Pheidippedes did his best. He galloped away, but by the time he reached his destination he wasn't feeling too bright. In fact he just about had enough strength left to cry, "Rejoice! We conquer!" before he collapsed and died. (If he'd done the same thing today he might have said "Flaming Olympics!" instead.)

The marathon isn't run over 280km nowadays, though. It's run over the most curious distance of 26 miles and 385 yards (42.2km),

It wasn't always this distance. In 1896 the marathon was a 25-mile race (40.2km). Then, in 1908, the Olympics were held in London and somebody thought it would be a good idea for the race to start at Windsor Castle. Inconveniently, Windsor Castle was 26 miles from the White City stadium, not 25 miles. Then, so the story goes, Princess Mary asked if the poor old runners could do another 385 yards so that they finished underneath the Royal Box. And everybody agreed! The 26 miles and 385 yards marathon was born.

NO, ONE CAN NOT MOVE ONE'S CASTLE DOWN THE ROAD A BIT!

MAKE YOUR OWN 'THE MARATHON' BOARD GAME

Actually running a marathon is pretty hard. So, why not do it the easy way and make your own Marathon Board Game to play instead? That way you'll get all the thrills but none of the agony. You'll need: one dice and a board 26 miles 385 yards long.

The idea is to take it in turns to throw the dice, moving yourself along the board by the appropriate number of spaces.

So first you've got to divide the board into 46,145 squares (one for each yard). Then, to make life interesting, put in the following penalty squares based on things that have really happened in Olympic marathons.

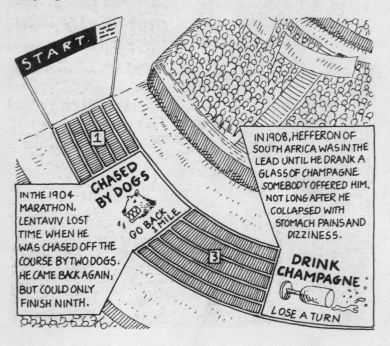

START.

1

IN THE 1904 MARATHON, LENTAVIV LOST TIME WHEN HE WAS CHASED OFF THE COURSE BY TWO DOGS. HE CAME BACK AGAIN, BUT COULD ONLY FINISH NINTH.

CHASED BY DOGS

"GO BACK 1 MILE"

IN 1908, HEFFERON OF SOUTH AFRICA WAS IN THE LEAD UNTIL HE DRANK A GLASS OF CHAMPAGNE SOMEBODY OFFERED HIM. NOT LONG AFTER HE COLLAPSED WITH STOMACH PAINS AND DIZZINESS.

3

DRINK CHAMPAGNE

LOSE A TURN

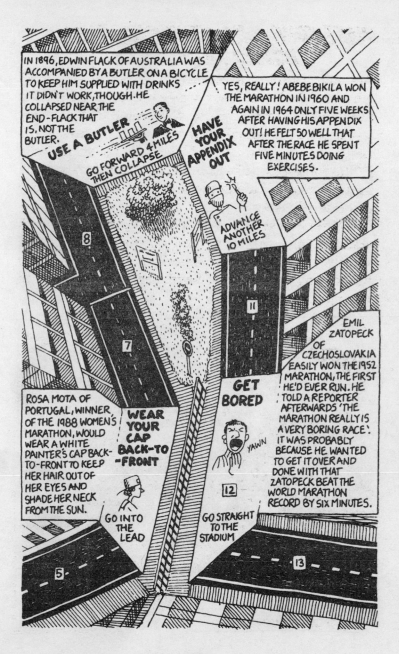

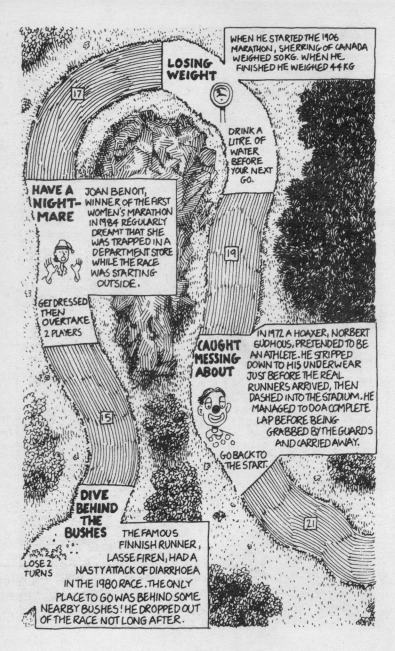

LOSING WEIGHT

WHEN HE STARTED THE 1906 MARATHON, SHERRING OF CANADA WEIGHED 50 KG. WHEN HE FINISHED HE WEIGHED 44 KG

DRINK A LITRE OF WATER BEFORE YOUR NEXT GO.

17

19

HAVE A NIGHTMARE

JOAN BENOIT, WINNER OF THE FIRST WOMEN'S MARATHON IN 1984 REGULARLY DREAMT THAT SHE WAS TRAPPED IN A DEPARTMENT STORE WHILE THE RACE WAS STARTING OUTSIDE.

GET DRESSED THEN OVERTAKE 2 PLAYERS

CAUGHT MESSING ABOUT

IN 1972 A HOAXER, NORBERT SUDHOUS, PRETENDED TO BE AN ATHLETE. HE STRIPPED DOWN TO HIS UNDERWEAR JUST BEFORE THE REAL RUNNERS ARRIVED, THEN DASHED INTO THE STADIUM. HE MANAGED TO DO A COMPLETE LAP BEFORE BEING GRABBED BY THE GUARDS AND CARRIED AWAY.

GO BACK TO THE START.

15

21

DIVE BEHIND THE BUSHES

THE FAMOUS FINNISH RUNNER, LASSE FIREN, HAD A NASTY ATTACK OF DIARRHOEA IN THE 1980 RACE. THE ONLY PLACE TO GO WAS BEHIND SOME NEARBY BUSHES! HE DROPPED OUT OF THE RACE NOT LONG AFTER.

LOSE 2 TURNS

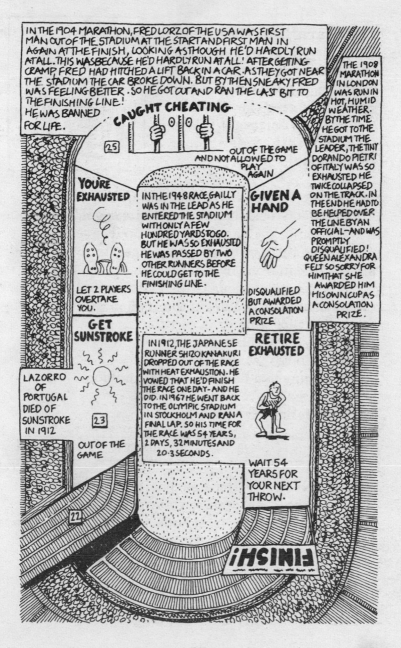

The Marathon Game Prize

The first player to get to the line is the winner. Of course, this being an Olympics game, you should give the winner a gold medal. You might like to come up with a few other prizes as well.

Question: In the first modern Games, held in Athens, the Greeks hadn't won a single gold medal. By the time it came to the final event, the marathon, they were getting desperate. Offers of prizes came in from all over the country. So, which of these prizes did various Greeks offer to any of their countrymen who could win the 1896 marathon?
  a) a barrel of wine
  b) 900kg of chocolate
  c) free shaves for life
  d) marriage to a daughter, plus 1 million drachmas
  e) free clothing for life

Answer: all of them!

Lo and behold – a Greek shepherd, Spiridon Louis, won the race! He promptly turned all the prizes down, saying he'd prefer a horse and cart instead.

Flaming Spectators

The stars of the Olympics are the competitors. But sometimes spectators can't resist joining in with the action themselves...

The Sporty Spartan

It happened in the ancient Olympics of course. Lichas, a Spartan, desperately wanted to win the chariot-race (the owner of the chariot and horses was proclaimed the winner, remember, not the chariot driver). The trouble was, Spartans weren't being allowed into the Games that year. So Lichas entered his chariot team under a false name and turned up to watch as a spectator.

So far, so good – until Lichas's team won the race. He couldn't contain his delight. Instead of staying undercover as a spectator, he charged across to the judges and claimed his prize. Twit. The judges spotted he was a Spartan at once. Instead of the laurel wreath he wanted, Lichas got a flogging instead.

Norbert the Nuisance

Like Lichas, Norbert Sudhous couldn't resist being part of the action either. His moment of fame came in 1972.

He was in the Olympic stadium. All around him, the crowd were eagerly awaiting the arrival of the leading runner in the marathon. So what did Norbert do? While everybody was looking the other way he...

- took off his jumper
- took off his shirt
- took off his trousers leaving him, in his vest and underpants, looking a bit like a runner. So next he
- jumped out on the track, and
- ran round pretending to be an athlete!

The crowd didn't realise for a while, and applauded him loudly as he ran most of the way round the track. Then, when they did realise, they booed him loudly. Finally the stadium guards grabbed Norbert and carried him away. They got the loudest cheer of all!

WHAT AN UNDIE-HAND TRICK!

The Paddling Papa

Another spectator went even further in 1952. Jean Boiteaux of France had just won the 400m freestyle when there was an almighty splash at the other end of the pool. A spectator had leapt in – not undressed, like Norbert Sudhous, but fully clothed! He'd even left his french beret on.

Before anybody could stop him, the spectator swam strongly across to Boiteaux. What did the new champion do? He took it all very calmly. He allowed the spectator to kiss him on both cheeks, then helped him out of the pool.

Surprising? Not really. The spectator was Boiteaux's father who'd seen his son's victory and just couldn't wait to congratulate him.

DAD, YOU'RE SUCH A DRIP!

These were all spectators who were supposed to have stayed in the crowd. Once, though, a spectator was actually asked to come out from the crowd and join in with the competition. It happened on 26 August, 1900...

The Super-Sub

"Papa," said the young boy, seeing his father putting on his hat and coat, "where are you going?"

"To the river, Philippe," said his father.

"Why?" asked Philippe. It was his favourite question.

His father smiled. "Because there are some rowing races taking place today."

"Why?"

"They are part of the Olympic Games, Philippe. The Games are being held here, in Paris."

"Why?"

"Oh, Philippe! Why not come with me and see for yourself?"

Philippe nodded eagerly and smiled happily at the same time. It always worked! If he asked enough questions, his father would suggest he came with him just to get some peace.

He skipped along as his father led the way from their small house and down to the banks of the River Seine. On this pleasant August day, the mighty river which ran right through Paris was smooth and calm.

Other people were hurrying in the same direction. Philippe looked out across the river.

"See the flags, Philippe?" said his father, pointing out at the rows of gaily-coloured flags dotted about on the water.

"What are they doing?" said Philippe, asking his second-favourite question.

"They are marking out the course for the rowing boats to follow."

Even as he said it, they heard the crash of the starter's gun. "Look, Philippe!" shouted the boy's father. "There they are!"

In the distance, away down the river, Philippe could just make out the three small rowing boats coming towards them. Each had two persons rowing, bending their backs as they pulled their oars strongly through the water. Each boat also had another person in it.

"That third one isn't rowing," said Philippe. He suddenly realised he hadn't used his favourite question for some time. "Why?"

"He is called the cox," said his father. "He doesn't row at all. His job is to steer the boat."

"An easy job, if you ask me!" said Philippe. "I could do that!" He had steered his father's small rowing boat on the river many a time.

They watched as the two leading boats went by, little between them. "I think it will be between those two in the final," said the boy's father. He began to move along the bank towards the finishing line. "Come on. Let's see them when they pull their boats from the water."

Philippe followed, dodging between the people going the same way. When they reached the finishing line, he ducked and weaved a bit more until he was at the front of the crowd.

"Here is the Dutch boat," his father said from behind him. "They came second. And they don't look too happy about it."

Philippe could see that for himself. The two rowers were shaking their heads and looking back angrily at the cox.

"He is too fat!" one was saying. "He slowed us down."

"I agree," said the other Dutch rower. "We will be second in the final too, unless we do something about it."

The first rower looked at his partner. "What?"

"Get him to lose some weight!" said the second rower, jerking a thumb towards their cox.

"Impossible! The final is this afternoon!"

"Then there's only one thing to do," said the first rower. "Find ourselves another cox."

"Another cox?"

"Yes, another cox. Somebody light! Somebody who can steer straight!"

The rowers looked at each other in despair. They shook their heads. It was hopeless. And then they heard a little voice from the front of the crowd.

"I'm light," said Philippe. "And I can steer straight."

After coming second in the heats, the two-man Dutch crew in the 1900 Olympic coxed pairs event changed their cox, Hermanus Brockman, for the final because they'd decided he was too heavy. In his place they used a French boy, taken from the spectators. The boy's name isn't known but he was between 7 and 10 years old and is the youngest-ever Olympic gold medal winner. With him as their cox, the Dutch team won the final by just 0.2 seconds!

Gotcha!

Finally, the tale of two spectators who wished they'd not bothered.

A couple of Brazilian volleyball fans were desperate to see their country's volleyball team compete in the 1992 Olympics in Barcelona. So, off they went to the stadium. The TV cameras were there, of course, beaming pictures back to those watching on TV in Brazil.

During a pause in the match, the cameras turned to show the faces in the crowd ... and the two fans were arrested shortly after. They were wanted crooks, who'd fled from Brazil owing £10 million!

PLAYING WITH FIRE: CHAMPION CHEATS

Athletes like to win (don't we all?) but some – and it's only a few – want to win so much that they'll try anything they can to gain an advantage. It's called cheating, and it's been going on since competitions began. The Greek poet, Homer, says even the Greek gods did it!

ODYSSEUS IS HAVING A RACE WITH AJAX. IT'S NECK-AND-NECK.
"OH, DEARSEUS," THINKS ODYSSEUS, "WHAT CAN I DO?" THERE'S ONLY ONE THING HE CAN THINK OF DOING, SO HE DOES IT. HE PRAYS TO THE GODDESS ATHENA FOR HELP.
"ATHENA, POLE-AXE THIS AJAX!"

LO AND BEHOLD (OR, RATHER, LOW AND BEHOLD) AJAX PROMPTLY SLIDES FACE FIRST INTO A PILE OF OX DUNG! ODYSSEUS WINS THE RACE!

A rather dirty trick, wouldn't you say? (Afterwards, of course, there was only one option left for poor old Ajax: to become a little cleaner!)

Following this good example, trickery and skulduggery went on at the ancient Games too. Even though the athletes promised to play fair at the opening ceremony, they still regularly practised these friendly little tricks. Can you match them with the event in which they were used?

a) Tripping and shoving as you went round the turning post.

1. Pankration

b) Rubbing sand in your opponent's eyes.

2. Chariot race

c) Biting

3. Foot-races

d) Bribing the judges to make you the winner even if you fall out and don't actually finish the race.

4. Wrestling

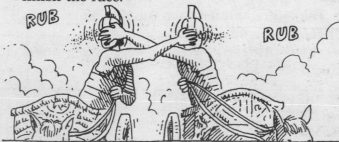

Answers: a) 3. (a trick which sent runners round the bend when it happened to them); b) 4. (as practised by particularly gritty performers); c) 1. (otherwise known as teething troubles); d) 2. (a speciality of the Emperor Nero, proving yet again what a big fiddler he was).

And that's the way it's been during the 100-year history of the modern Olympics, too. Competitors have carried on playing tricks to help them win. Some of the tricks have been sneaky, some have been mean, some have been dirty – and some have been sneaky, mean *and* dirty! Here are a few...

Bribery

As usual, the ancient Olympics led the way in this. Without any TV cameras taking close-ups or photo-finishes, decisions were all down to the judges. So bribing a judge to say you'd won your race was one way of winning. The other way was to bribe your opponent. The earliest case of this took place in 388BC when a boxer named Eupolus bribed three other boxers to let him win.

What was the punishment for somebody who was found guilty of bribery?

a) They paid a fine.
b) They were banned from future Games.
c) They received a flogging.
d) Their title and wreath were taken away if they'd won their event.

IT'S THE WINNERS WHIPPING SESSION!

Answer: a) or b) or c) could be right, but d) is definitely wrong! Amazingly, somebody who'd used bribery to win their event wasn't disqualified but allowed to remain the winner!

Usually the cheat had to pay a fine, the money being used to erect a statue to Zeus. On the bottom would be a message saying something like: "Olympic champions win with speed and strength, not money." This sounds pretty good, but as the cheat was still allowed to remain the winner it also sounds pretty daft!

Here Comes The Judge!

There have been cases in the modern Olympics where the judges haven't needed to be bribed, they've volunteered to cheat (well, not exactly cheat perhaps – just not stick to the rules)! At the opening ceremony the judges promise not to take sides. But what would you say these did...

● A 10th anniversary Games were held in Athens in 1906. There, a Greek runner named George Bonhag had been expected to win both the 1,500 metres and 5-mile running races but he'd failed miserably in both. So at the last minute he entered the 1,500 metre walk – and won that! Everybody was surprised – but none more than the race favourites who'd all been disqualified by the judges for one reason or another!

109

- In the 1908 middleweight boxing final, Reg Baker (AUS) accused the judge of being biased towards the winner, John Douglas (GB). The judge denied it ... even though his surname was Douglas and he was the winner's father!
- Another famous case occurred in 1952, at the end of the 10km walk. In a tight finish for second place a Swiss, Fritz Schwab, and a Russian, Bruno Junk, were neck and neck (well, toe and toe). They got faster ... and faster ... until, 30km from the line they forget all about walking and started running. What happened? The biased judges (who were very anti-Russia) said they hadn't seen anything wrong – even though the "walkers" had outsprinted the judges to the finishing line!
- Things hadn't improved by 1988 in Seoul, where an amazingly high number of Korean boxers managed to score wins. After one bout, in which Park Si-Hun of Korea was judged to have beaten Roy Jones (USA), a number of the judges were suspended. Jones was later awarded a cup as the best boxer in the Games!

False Starts

The most common type of cheating in a running race is the false start – that is, trying to get away before the starter's gun goes off.

What punishment did you receive if you were guilty of a false start at the ancient Games?

a) You had to pay a fine.
b) You were banned from future Games.

c) You received a flogging.
d) Your title and wreath were taken away if they'd won their event.

THIS IS AN ODD STAGGERED START!

THAT'S BECAUSE IT'S A STAGGERING-HEAD-START !!!

Answer: c) Yes, in those days the punishment fitted the crime. If you'd beaten the starter, the starter had you beaten!

In the modern Olympics, the rule is two false starts and you're disqualified. But this rule has changed over the years. In 1904 a runner had to go back by about 2 metres for every false start he made. This was dead handy for the USA sprinter Archie Hahn. There were three other runners in his race – and they all had false starts, one after the other! Hahn won the gold medal.

Sometimes, though, the judges have a tricky decision to make. See if you can get this one right. It happened to a Russian named Rapp in the 1,000m cycling time trial in 1972...

1. Before the pistol went, Rapp started moving.
2. Realising he'd made a false start, and thinking he'd be ordered to start again, Rapp stopped.

What happened next?

(upside-down answer box at top)

Answer: Rapp was disqualified – but not for the false start. The judges hadn't spotted that, so they disqualified Rapp for stopping. (A clear case of an innocent man taking the Rapp for something he didn't do!)

Punch-Ups

Fighting your opponent is sometimes allowed – but not when you're supposed to be in a running race! In the ancient Games, though, it happened all the time. The runners in the 2-stade and 24-stade races didn't have to stay in lanes or anything like that, they just had to charge down the track and go round the posts which were positioned at each end. Take your pick from this list of what runners weren't supposed to do to each other – but did!

- Tripping (another one bites the dust!)

- Holding (nasty, they were all naked remember)

- Running in front of somebody (so that he ran into the post)

- Going inside, not outside, the post (first example of taking a short cut)

I Say, That's Not British!

Believe it or not, a similar problem occurred in the 1908 Games 400m race. At that time there were no lanes going round the track. Four runners were in the race, three from the USA and one, Wyndham Halswelle, from Britain. As they entered the finishing straight it was neck and neck between Halswelle and Carpenter, one of the Americans. As Halswelle tried to overtake, Carpenter moved out and blocked his path. The officials' decision was that the race should be run again.

What do you think happened in the re-run?

a) Carpenter won.

b) Halswelle won.

c) Neither of them won.

HEY, WHY AREN'T YOU WATCHING?

BECAUSE IT'S A NO-ACTION REPLAY

Answer: b) Halswelle won – running on his own! Carpenter refused to run again, and the other two Americans walked out with him. In the history of Olympic athletics, this is the only time there's been a walk-over. (Why not a run-over?) Ever since, the running track has been divided into lanes all the way round.

Even More Punch-Ups

The events in which punch-ups are supposed to take place still give plenty of opportunities for cheating, though. Which of these were boxers allowed to do in the ancient Games, and which are they allowed to do now?

a) Hitting the back of the neck (called a rabbit punch, because it's the method used to kill a rabbit).

b) Hitting below the belt.

c) Hitting with the heel of the hand.

d) Hitting a man on the ground.

e) Hitting with the teeth (biting, in other words!).

f) Gouging – that is, poking your thumb in the other man's eye and pulling it out (your thumb and his eye!).

Answers: Boxing in the ancient Games allowed a) b) c) and d), but not e) and f). In modern boxing, none of them are allowed.

"Tell that to the judge!" might have been the cry of Harry Mallin, in 1924. He was defending his middleweight title against a Frenchman named Roger Brousse and lost on points. What did Mallin immediately claim that the Frenchman had done to him during the fight?

a) Kissed him on both cheeks.

b) Whispered rude words in his ear.

c) Bitten him on the chest.

Answer: c) whereupon the judges examined Mallin's chest and found the teethmarks. Mallin was awarded the fight and went on to win the gold medal again.

How about this one, concerning two French cyclists? In the 1936 cycling road race over 100km, Guy Lapebic was just in front of Robert Charpentier as they raced for the finishing line. Suddenly, Lapebic slowed down – and Charpentier went past him to win by a fraction of a second. What had happened to Lapebic?

a) Wheel trouble.
b) Back trouble.
c) Pedal trouble.

Answer: b) Charpentier had grabbed his shirt, and pulled him back!

Fixing the Equipment

In the ancient Games it was a case of fixing the judges or your opponents. Nowadays, with the arrival of timing equipment and cameras, it's not so easy to cheat. But some have tried...

Glow Home, Boris!

In fencing, for instance, a lot of the judging is done electronically. Fencers wear breastplates which are wired up, as are their swords. This way, when one fencer's sword hits the other's breastplate a light on the judges' table comes on.

Boris Onyschenko, a Russian, tried to fix the equipment in 1976. His aim was to fool the judges into thinking he'd scored a hit when he hadn't. The trouble was, he fixed things too well. The light came on before he'd got near enough to reach his opponent! What happened to him? He was told to go home, of course!

Getting a Grip on Things

In another famous case, the equipment got fixed later. Harold Osborn (USA), the winner of the 1924 high jump, had a very interesting technique. It was:

1. run in;
2. take off;
3. use a hand to press the bar back against the high-jump post so that it didn't fall off if he whacked it on the way over;
4. land.

He managed a (then) Olympic record leap of 1.98 metres using this method – which wasn't against the rules. Afterwards, though, the design of the high jump posts was changed so that the pegs on which the bar rested were inside them, rather than at the back of them. Osborn's technique couldn't be used any more.

Pills and Potions

In the history of the modern Games, over 50 competitors have been caught taking drugs to make their performance better.

Many of them have been weightlifters and wrestlers, who take drugs to give them extra strength. Some have been taking part in shooting events, using drugs that would calm their nerves and keep their hands steady. Others, such as cyclists and runners, use drugs to gain extra power and speed.

In their desire to win, they ignore the dangers of taking drugs. And the dangers are very real. In the 1960 Games, the Danish cyclist Knut Jensen died because of the drugs he'd taken.

Of all the drugs cases, though, none caused more of a scandal than that of the Canadian sprinter Ben Johnson in 1988. In the 100m final Johnson had rocketed from his starting blocks to win the race in a world-record time, his arch-rival Carl Lewis (USA) beaten into second place.

Johnson received his gold medal and, like all medalists, was drugs-tested. His test proved that he'd been taking drugs called steroids, to give him extra power. Johnson was immediately disqualified and his gold medal awarded to Lewis.

He had been "the fastest man in the world" for only two days.

Who, me...?

The rules about drugs are very strict, and sometimes athletes can take them almost without knowing.

The swimmer Rick Demont (USA) was disqualified after winning the 400m free-style in 1972, even though he hadn't deliberately taken drugs. He was an asthma sufferer, and the drug was in the inhalant he used.

It's pretty dumb for an athlete to take drugs anyway, but it's doubly dumb when they don't help at all! The oldest Olympic competitor to be caught taking drugs so far has been Paul Cerutti of Monaco, who was 65 years old when he took part in the 1972 trap shooting event. He was disqualified, of course, although it didn't affect the result. He'd come 43rd out of 44!

When you've got to go, you've got to go!

Drug-taking is a serious business, but it does have its funny side.

Imagine you've just won an Olympic gold medal. This is what happens with a drugs test.

What's more the official won't go away until he's got what he came for, however long you take between steps **4.** and **5.** Sometimes he's had rather a long wait though...

The Boxing Boozer

In 1968, Chris Finnegan (GB) won the middle-weight boxing gold. Into the loo he went with his bottle – and didn't come out! He couldn't manage a drop! The officials sent out for a pint of beer. He still couldn't manage anything. They sent for another pint of beer ... and another ... and another ... Early next morning, Finnegan finally came out with something in his bottle. He'd had to drink eight pints!

The Running Dribbler

The runner Rod Dixon (NZE) had a similar problem after managing third place in the 1972 1,500m race. After staying in the loo for some time, he sheepishly put his head round the door and handed out his bottle. It had the merest dribble in the bottom. "Will it do?" he asked. The official frowned, then finally nodded. "For a gold medal, no. But for a bronze, it will do."

The Finnish Vampire

Drug-taking is about putting something false into your body to help you perform better. But what if you put something of your own into your body? Well, that's allowed, and the Finnish runner Lasse Viren was the most famous athlete accused of doing it. Doing what? Using his own blood...

This is how. (Readers, do not try this at home. It can make an awful mess in kitchen.)

- He was supposed to have taken 1 litre of blood (his own)...
- Put it in the freezer...

121

- Then had a lie down until his body had made enough new blood to fill him up again.
- Just before his next race, he'd taken the frozen blood out of the freezer (making sure it was his blood and not a bag of blackcurrent ice-lollies)...
- De-frosted it...
- Injected it back into his body...
- Then gone off and run his race.

This is called "blood-boosting", and the idea is that, with an extra litre of blood inside you, your body will have far greater endurance than normal.

It sounds nasty, and Viren always denied that he used blood-boosting. The newspapers weren't so sure. They knew that the technique was developed in Viren's part of the world, and always thought it supsicious that he managed to be at his best for the major championships. Viren claimed it was good training.

Whatever the truth, he was certainly a brilliant athlete. Lasse Viren won both the 5,000m and 10,000m gold medals in 1972 and 1976.

Who are you – and WHAT are you?

Remember Kallpateira, the woman who sneaked in to watch the ancient Games dressed as a man because women weren't allowed? After this all competitors and trainers had to appear naked when they were entering events so that any woman posing as a man would be spotted at once!

In the modern Olympics, sex-testing as it is called, has been in force since 1968. But, unlike the Kallipateira case, it's not designed to reveal women pretending to be men, but the other way round – to discover women athletes who are really men. A lot of women object to this testing, saying that it is unfair and unnecessary. Against them, others argue that it makes sure everybody is equal.

Mind you, pretending to be a woman hasn't always been a good idea. At the 1936 Games a woman high-jumper named Dora Ratjen was found to be a man posing as a woman. It hadn't done him much good, though – he'd only come fourth!

Gamesmanship & Sportsmanship

Question – When is cheating not cheating?

Answer – When it's gamesmanship! (Or gameswomanship – women do it just as well.)

Gamesmanship is doing something which is in the rules but which puts your opponents off in some way, either by ruining their concentration or making them feel inferior in some way.

Zato the Rat-o

The brilliant Czech runner Emil Zatopeck was really ace at this. In the 1952 marathon, the first he'd ever entered, he was well in the lead after 15 miles but slowed down to let Jim Peters (GB) catch him up.

When Peters, who was one of the favourites to win the race, came gasping along, Zatopeck said to him:

I HAVEN'T RUN A MARATHON BEFORE, BUT... DON'T YOU THINK WE OUGHT TO GO FASTER?

And with that he shot off to win, leaving Peters feeling all petered out.

A good sport

Sportsmanship is the opposite to gamesmanship. It's doing something to make your opponent feel better, not worse – like the 800m runner Eby (USA) in 1920 who accidentally bumped into Rudd (SFA) and turned round to say "Sorry!"

The "Gamesman or Sportsman?" Test

So, are you a gamesman or a sportsman? Try this quiz to find out. All the questions are based on actual incidents that happened in the Olympics.

1. You're Harold Abrahams in 1924, and you've been entered for the 100m and the long jump. You want to concentrate on the 100m. Do you:

   a) do your best in both anyway

   b) write a letter to the newspapers saying it was stupid picking you for the long jump, so that you can then show it to the people picking the team and ask to be excused?

2. You're McCarthur, running with Gilsham in the 1912 marathon. He says he's going to stop for a drink at the next refreshment point. You say you'll wait for him. Do you:

   a) wait for him, like you said

   b) shoot off while he's having his drink?

3. You're Duquesne of France, racing against Nurmi of Finland in the 1928 steeplechase. Nurmi has never run this race before and he falls at a hurdle. Do you:
  a) stop and help him up
  b) tread on him?

4. Now you're Nurmi, in the same race. It's the finishing straight, and you're neck and neck with Duquesne. Do you:
  a) let him win because of what he did to you
  b) try to beat the socks off him because of what he did to you?

5. You're Emil Zatopeck in the 1952 10,000m race. You're well in the lead, and feel great. Do you:
  a) keep going
  b) start wobbling and gasping and generally pretend you're dying until the others catch you up, then shoot off into the lead again?

6. You're Paavo Nurmi again, this time running in the 1920 10,000m. Do you:
  a) look at the other runners with respect
  b) show you don't expect anybody else to keep up with you by carrying a stop-watch in your hand to see how fast you're going?

7. You're Guillemot, running in the same 1920 10,000m race as Nurmi. He beats you. As you cross the finishing line, do you:

   a) shake his hand

   b) throw up all over him?

8. You're Ralph Craig, at the starting line for the 1912 100m. False starts aren't allowed, but you don't get disqualified if you make one. Do you:

   a) wait for the gun before moving

   b) make as many false starts as you can to be sure of getting away well?

9. You're Luz Long of Germany, in the 1936 long jump. Your country's dictator, Adolf Hitler, has said you must beat Jesse Owens, a black American athlete. He's had two no-jumps. One more, and he's out of the competition. Do you:

   a) give him some helpful advice

   b) give him some unhelpful advice?

10. You're Bill Henry, the American stadium announcer at the 1932 Games in Los Angeles. Lehtinen (FIN) has just beaten your country's runner, Hill, in the 5,000m final after deliberately blocking him twice during the race. The crowd are booing. Do you:

   a) ask the crowd to stop booing

   b) join in, booing through your loudspeaker?

What really happened:

1. b) Harold Abrahams (GB) was chosen for both events in 1924. He wrote a letter to the Daily Express, didn't do the long jump – and won the 100m.

2. b) McCarthur buzzed off – and won.

3. a) Duquesne stopped and helped Nurmi up.

4. a) Nurmi allowed Duquesne to win.

5. b) Zatopeck wobbled, gasped etc – and still managed to beat the world record by 42 seconds.

6. b) Nurmi did this in every race he ran, only throwing it infield when he started his final spurt for the finishing line.

7. b) To be fair, the race had been brought forward four hours at short notice and Guillemot had already eaten.

8. b) Craig had three false starts (nowadays he'd have been disqualified after two). He wasn't alone, though. There were seven false starts before the race was finally started for Craig to win.

9. a) Long suggested that Owen draw a line a few inches back from the take-off board and aim for that so as to be sure of getting in a good jump. Owens did as Long suggested, qualified for the final, and then won the gold medal with a world-record jump. Luz Long came second.

10. a) Henry quietened the crowd by saying, "Remember, these people are our guests."

How did you score?

More a) than b) You're a real sportsman.

About equal a) and b) You're a sport, but not all the time.

More b) than a) You need to be watched.

All b) I'd trust you as far as I could throw you with both hands tied behind my back!

BLAZING ROWS – FLAMING OLYMPIC DISASTERS

As in every competition, not everybody can be a winner. Some have to lose. But here are some Olympic competitors who didn't even get to take part! Try and guess why.

Miruts Yifter of Ethiopia turned up too late for his heat of the 5,000m in 1972. Was it because:

1. he spent too long on the toilet
2. he got lost
3. he went to the wrong check-in gate stadium?

Answer: Nobody knows for sure, but it was rumoured to be all three! No wonder his nickname was Yifter the Shifter!

Essajas of Surinam missed his 800m first-round heat in 1960. Did he:

1. have a watch that stopped
2. get told the wrong time for his heat
3. spend too long in bed?

Robinson and **Hart** (both USA) missed their 100m semi-final in 1972. It was in the afternoon, not the evening as they thought. How did they find out the bad news?

1. They read about it in the evening newspaper.
2. They saw the race on television.
3. They received a telephone call from the President of the United States

Mary Decker of the United States, was world-record holder and red-hot favourite for a 3,000m gold medal but something stopped her. Did it happen in:

1. 1976
2. 1980
3. 1984

Answer: All three! Mary Decker's luck was right out where the Olympics were concerned. In 1976 she was injured; in 1980 the USA team was withdrawn; and when she finally got to run in 1984 she tripped over Zola Budd in her first-round heat and failed to finish.

Ten Melting Moments

Mary Decker's disaster was just one of the many which litter Olympic history. They've been happening ever since that embarassed runner lost his shorts in the "running-in-armour race" at the ancient Games (see page 81–83 for the bare facts!). His disaster, like Mary Decker's, was total. Neither of them managed to recover. Others have suffered disasters, though, and gone on to win medals.

See if you can work out the answers in this absolute disaster of a quiz!

1. The Cuban runner Feliz Carvajal set off for America in 1904. He wanted to run in the marathon, and he'd raised all his own money for the fare. **Disaster! What happened next?**

2. There was just 15 minutes to go before Charles

Vinci of the United States had his weight checked for the 1956 bantamweight section of the weightlifting. **Disaster!** He found he was 200 grams too heavy! **What happened next?**

3. Rasmuson of Sweden needed to beat Masala of Italy in the 4,000 metres race, the last event of the 1984 Modern Pentathlon. On the last bend, Rasmuson was just ahead when ... **Disaster! What happened next?**

4. Marjorie Jackson of Australia was after her third gold medal of the 1952 Games. As she set off to run the last leg of the 4 x 100m relay, Australia were just ahead when ... **Disaster! What happened next?**

5. The cyclist, Coekelburg, was leading in the 1908 100km cycle race when **Disaster!** A judge stepped into his path and made him crash. A few days later, Coekelburg was in the 10-miles race when ... **Double disaster! What happened this time?**

6. In 1988, Greg Louganis of Canada was trying to win the springboard diving event for the second time. He leapt up in the air and ... **Disaster! What happened next?**

7. Noel, of France, was competing in the 1932 discus final. Winding himself up, he launched the furthest throw of the competition. **Disaster! It wasn't allowed! Why not?**

8. Jindrich Suoboda was raring to play for Czechoslovakia against East Germany in the 1980 Olympic football final. But ... **Disaster! He was only named as substitute. What happened next?**

9. In the 1924 rapid-fire pistol shooting, Bailey of USA was shooting in a tie-break for the gold medal. He had to fire six shots in ten seconds. The clock started, and ... **Disaster! Bailey's gun jammed. What happened next?**

10. Sue Platt of Great Britain watched as her third round throw in the 1960 javelin competition soared away to land in the silver medal position. Then ... **Disaster! What happened next?**

1. Carjaval lost all his money in a card game and had to hitch-hike the rest of the way, just managing to arrive in time for the start. He was still wearing heavy shoes, long trousers and a beret! Somebody cut the legs off his trousers to turn them into shorts, and away Felix went. He managed to come fourth!

2. Vinci lost the extra 200 grams by having a very short haircut – and went on to win the gold medal.

3. Rasmuson fell over a potted plant at the side of the track! Masala overtook him and won the gold medal by just 13 points.

4. Marjorie dropped the baton and Australia came nowhere.

5. Another judge stepped in front of Coekelburg and he crashed again!

6. Louganis hit his head on the diving board. But Louganis was a tough nut. He completed the rest of his dives – and won the gold medal!

7. Because all the judges had been watching the pole vault! They gave Noel another throw, but it was nothing like as good as his other one and he came fourth instead of first. Definitely hell for Noel!

8. Suoboda came on with 19 minutes to go and scored the only goal of the game!

9. Bailey calmly unloaded the dud cartridge and fired off five perfect shots in the time he had left. His opponent missed two of his six, and Bailey won the gold.

10. Sue Platt jumped for joy – and stepped over the foul line by mistake! The throw was disallowed and she couldn't manage another one as good. She came fourth, missing out on the medals.

Woe is Me!

It's obvious what you do when you become a champion. You shout with joy, you laugh, you run a lap of honour.

But what about when you lose?

What do *you* do when things don't go right – for instance, when you're expecting to win the sack race but end up landing on your nose six times and finishing second from last? Do you jump up and down (which is what you should have been doing anyway!) or scream and shout? Do you go home and sulk? Knock the stuffing out of your teddy bear? Teach the parrot rude words?

Olympic failures have done some peculiar things...

Short back and sides

• In 1964 Elvira Ozolina (URS) failed to win the javelin title she'd won in 1960. She was so disgusted with herself that she marched straight into a hairdressers and had her head shaved.

• Maybe she'd watched the Japanese wrestling team in 1960. After a collection of poor performances they *all* went and had their heads shaved!

Ending it all

• Another Japanese went tragically further. In 1960, with the Games being held in Tokyo, Kokichi Tsuburaya felt that he'd let his whole country down by only coming third in the marathon (particularly as he'd been overtaken in the stadium itself). He felt his only way of redeeming himself was to win the marathon at the next Games in 1964. When he injured himself and realised he wouldn't be able to take part, he committed suicide.

● Another case of suicide also involved a marathon runner. Ens Fast (SWE) ran in the 1900 marathon in Paris. This race was run over a very complicated route, and Ens got lost. So, what do you do when you get lost? You ask a policeman to tell you the way. Just what Ens did – only to be told the wrong way! Enough to make anybody suicidal, you might think ... except that it wasn't Ens Fast who killed himself. It was the policeman. Afterwards he was teased about this incident so much that he shot himself. Remember this tragic story next time you're tempted to tease somebody...

Ahoy there!

But, for a really spectacular exhibition of the miseries, there's been little to beat what the British yachtsmen Alan Warren and David Hunt did in 1976.

After their yacht broke down for the third time they set fire to it – then sat in a dinghy to watch it burn! Only when it finally sank to the bottom of Lake Ontario were they satisfied. (I bet they were muttering about "flaming Olympics", too.)

Flare-Ups: Flaming Olympic Disputes

In the ancient Games the winner of an event got the olive wreath and the title of champion. But what did those who came second and third get?

a) Nothing
b) A handshake from the chief judge
c) A certificate
d) A picture of an olive wreath

Answer: a) Nothing. Only winners got prizes in the ancient Games.

In the Olympics, winning has always been all-important. That means that in a close contest there'll always be arguments about who's actually won. And in the Olympics there have been plenty of arguments!

Usually, the judges are in the middle of things. After all, settling arguments is what they're there for. But sometimes they're the cause of the argument...

● In the 1920 football final, Belgium were beating Czechoslovakia 2-0 when the Czechs walked off because they thought the referee was being unfair.

PHEEP! PHEEP!

THE REF'S TRYING TO SEND THEM ON!

● In the 1972 basketball final, the USA were beating Russia by one point with one second to go when the judges decided that the clock was wrong. They had it put back by two seconds ... giving Russia enough time to score the winning basket and stop USA winning the basketball gold for the first time ever.

● The judges decided that Devitt (AUS) had just beaten Larson (USA) in the 1960 100m freestyle swimming. The result had to stand – even though the electronic timing devices made Larson 0.1 seconds faster! (After this dispute, electronic times were always used to decide the results of swimming events.)

Silent Protests

Sometimes, the best way of protesting is to say nothing – but just get on and win. Here are some who did just that – eventually.

- In 1906, the USA 400m runner Paul Pilgrim wasn't picked for the American Team. So he paid his own fare to Athens, and won!
- Forrest Smithson was a Theology student who, in 1908, objected to the final of the 110m hurdles being held on a Sunday. His way of protesting was to run, but with a Bible in his left hand. He won, in world record time.
- A similar case was that of the Scottish runner, Eric Liddell, whose story was told in the film *Chariots of Fire*. He wouldn't run in his 100m heat on a Sunday, full stop. So he ran on another day in the 400m instead – and won it in an Olympic record time.

Seconds out!

Finally, there was the case of the silent protest which didn't do any good.

● In 1988, the Korean boxer Byun Jong-Il was penalised for butting. After losing his bout he staged a sit-down protest, refusing to leave the ring. He stayed put for 67 minutes (enough time to have fought another 22 rounds), but the judges didn't change their minds.

OH, BLOW! – THE CLOSING CEREMONY

The Olympics open with a great ceremony. They close with one too. So did the ancient Games. In those days the ceremony amounted to:

- prize-giving of olive wreaths to the champions (but nothing to the runners-up, remember)
- giving of thanks to Zeus for looking after the Games
- a winner's banquet, at which the sacrificial oxen were cooked and everybody ate every body

For the modern Olympics in 1896 things on the final day were pretty much the same, apart from the fact that nobody gave thanks to Zeus and there weren't any oxen to eat and this time the runners-up did get something...

- Champions got a silver medal (not gold) and a crown of olive leaves.
- Runners-up got a bronze medal and a crown of laurel leaves.

Over the years, though, the medal-giving ceremonies and the closing ceremony have separated. Now, medals are awarded to first, second and third soon after the event has finished in a ceremony that finishes with the national anthem of the winner's country.

Did You Know?
- Bronze medals for third-placed contestants were awarded for the first time in 1908.
- Until 1928 all the medals were given out at the closing ceremony on the last day.
- In the early years, winners of team events (for instance, 4 x 100m relay in athletics) had to share one medal.

- The victory stand, with its 1 – 2 – 3 positions, was introduced in 1932.
- An olympic gold medal is only worth about £75. This is because over 90% of it isn't gold at all, but solid silver. There's only 6 grammes of gold covering it – and that's worth more on the medal than off!

Gimme me medal!

You might think that nothing much could go wrong at a medal-giving ceremony. Wrong! There have been some red faces throughout the history of the Games...

What happened next?

1. 1912. Jim Thorpe (USA) stands ready to receive his medal from King Gustav V of Sweden. The King says to Thorpe, "Sir, you are the greatest athlete in the world." Jim Thorpe says...

2. 1924. Harold Abrahams (GB) hears a rattle at his letterbox. There's a package on the mat. He opens it. Out drops...

3. 1936. Japanese pole vaulters Shuhei Nishada and Sueu Oe finish equal second in the pole vault. They refuse to jump off for second and third places, but there is only one silver medal and one bronze...

4. 1956. Rower Vyacheslav Ivanov (URS) is so excited about winning his medal he throws it in the air – but fails to catch it...

5. 1964. Abebe Bikila receives his gold medal for winning the Marathon. The Ethiopian flag begins to rise as the band strikes up...

6. 1972. Dave Wottle (USA), who always runs in an

old golf cap, receives his medal for the 800m. The American anthem strikes up, and Wottle turns solemnly towards the flag ...

Answers:
1. "Thanks, King!"
2. His 100m gold medal. There were no presentation ceremonies at the 1924 Games.
3. They took them home to Japan where they asked a jeweller to cut the medals in half, then weld them together so that they both had a medal that was half silver and half bronze!
4. And it plopped into the waters of Lake Wendouree! Ivanov was given another one. (Attention Australian treasure hunters: the original medal has never been found!)
5. And plays the Japanese national anthem! The band didn't know the Ethiopian anthem.
6. But forgets to take his cap off. He appeared on TV later, crying as he apologised to the American public.

The Closing Ceremony

Here we are then, at the closing ceremony. It's a grand affair, with lots going on. Which of the following *won't* you expect to see?

- Flag bearers of national flags and six team members from each country parading into the stadium.
- All the other competitors coming in together to show that they're united in sport.

- Three national anthems being played – of Greece, of the host country, and of the country to be hosts next time.

- A closing speech being made (of course!).
- The mayor of the city hosting the next Games receiving the ceremonial Olympic flag to look after.
- The Olympic flame being extinguished.
- The Olympic flag that has flown throughout the Games being taken down and paraded out of the Stadium.
- A UFO landing in the middle of the arena.

Answer: They all usually happen except the last one...

But in 1984 in Los Angeles a UFO landed too, right in the middle of the arena. Out stepped an "alien"...

Except that – surprise! surprise! – he wasn't a real alien. He was actually a student, specially chosen for what the organisers thought were his alien looks: he was 7ft 8ins (2.44m) tall! His job was to emphasize what a good thing the Olympic Games had been by saying: "I've come a long way, because I like what I've seen!"

After The Games Are Over...

What do Olympic athletes do when the Games are over? Some, of course, carry on competing. There are National Championships, European Championships, Etc. Etc. Championships and World Championships in most sports nowadays.

But what about life outside sport? Many competitors go back to their jobs. Some go on to do other things. See how you get on with this final quiz about Olympic competitors and what they got up to after they'd finished competing...

1. The 1900 marathon champion returned to his job working for:
   a) a butcher
   b) a baker
   c) a candlestick maker

2. The 1920 middleweight boxing champion returned to his job as:
   a) a policeman
   b) a bus driver
   c) a road sweeper

3. The winner of five swimming gold medals in 1924 and 1928 went on to star in more than a dozen films as:
   a) Tarzan
   b) Superman
   c) Batman

4. The 1924 men's 400m champion became:
   a) a vicar in London

b) a monk in Tibet

c) a missionary in China

5. The winner of a silver medal for weightlifting in 1948 later tried to do something very unpleasant to James Bond. Was it:

a) slice him in half with a laser beam

b) cut his head off

c) tuck him up in bed with a tarantula

6. The 1960 Decathlon gold medallist later became:

a) an actor

b) a pop singer

c) a bodyguard

7. A member of a 1976 Equestrian team went home and continued to be:

a) the wife to another equestrian team member

b) a princess

c) the daughter of somebody very famous

Answers:

1. b) Michel Theato (FRA) worked as a baker's roundsman.

2. a) Harry Mallin (GB) was a policeman.

150

3. a) Johnny Weismuller (USA) made a highly successful switch from swimming between ropes to swinging from them!

4. c) After his famous stand against running on a Sunday, Eric Liddell (GB) went on to be a missionary.

5. b) Harold Sakata (USA) later played the meanie "Oddjob" in the James Bond film *Goldfinger* in which he tried to cut the hero's head off with his steel-edged bowler hat.

6. a) and c) Rafer Johnson became an actor (appearing with Elvis Presley in one film – but with Elvis doing the singing) and then bodyguard to Senator Robert Kennedy.

7. All three! HRH Princess Anne was married to Captain Mark Phillips, who competed for Great Britain in 1972 and 1976. They divorced in 1991, but she has continued to be a princess and the daughter of somebody very famous.

Last, but not least, there's the world-famous Briton who won a bronze in the super-heavyweight wrestling. Everybody knew what he looked like, but hardly anybody knew that his name was Ken Richmond.

Even you probably know what he looks like, but I bet you don't know his name is Ken Richmond either.

Why? Because he's the strongman who whacks the gong at the start of the old films on TV.

Beat that if you can!

Atlanta 1996: The Flaming Centenary Olympics

Like the "alien" who turned up at the closing ceremony in 1984, I hope you've liked what you've seen in this book.

Of course the thing about the Olympics is that there is always another flaming one round the corner, providing more champs and chumps, disputes and disasters.

So, why not tune in and make a note of the things you spot? Who knows, you could be writing your own *Flaming Olympics* book in time for the next Games. They're being held in Sydney in the year 2000.

So, come on. Start thinking of a title. *Ozzie Olympics? The Neighbourly Games? The Sydney Sprints?* Over to you, Mr Starter!

VENUES OF SUMMER OLYMPIADS

① **GREECE**
1ST 1896 ATHENS
1NT 1906 ATHENS

② **FRANCE**
2ND 1900 PARIS
8TH 1924 PARIS

③ **USA**
3RD 1904 ST. LOUIS
10TH 1932 LOS ANGELES
23RD 1984 LOS ANGELES
26TH 1996 ATLANTA

④ **GREAT BRITAIN**
4TH 1908 LONDON
13TH 1944 LONDON (CANCELLED)
14TH 1948 LONDON

⑤ **SWEDEN**
5TH 1912 STOCKHOLM

⑥ **GERMANY**
6TH 1916 BERLIN (CANCELLED)
11TH 1936 BERLIN
20TH 1972 MUNICH

⑦ **BELGIUM**
7TH 1920 ANTWERP

⑧ **HOLLAND**
9TH 1928 AMSTERDAM

⑨ **JAPAN**
12TH 1940 TOKYO (CANCELLED)
18TH 1964 TOKYO

⑩ **FINLAND**
15TH 1952 HELSINKI

⑪ **AUSTRALIA**
16TH 1956 MELBOURNE

⑫ **ITALY**
17TH 1960 ROME

⑬ **MEXICO**
19TH 1960 MEXICO CITY

⑭ **CANADA**
21ST 1976 MONTREAL

⑮ **RUSSIA**
22ND 1980 MOSCOW

⑯ **SOUTH KOREA**
24TH 1988 SEOUL

⑰ **SPAIN**
25TH 1992 BARCELONA

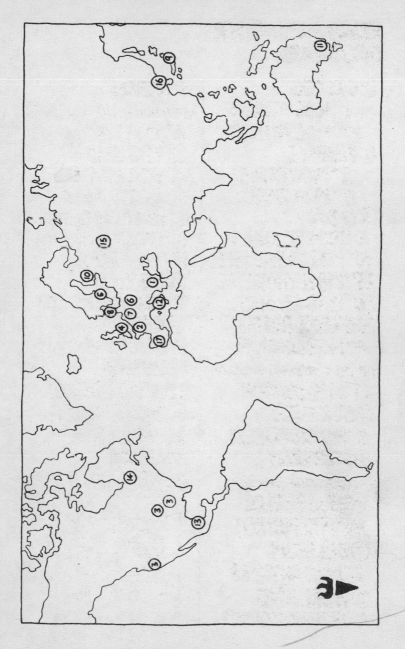

by Terry Deary

The Terrible Tudors
The Awesome Egyptians
The Vile Victorians
The Rotten Romans
The Vicious Vikings
The Blitzed Brits
The Groovy Greeks
The Slimy Stuarts
Horrible Histories Special:
Cruel Kings and Mean Queens

Coming soon:

Dreadful Diary
Horrible Histories Special: Wicked Words
Horrible Histories Special: The 20th Century
The Measly Middle Ages
The Cut-throat Celts

History has never been so horrible!

HORRIBLE SCIENCE

Science with the squishy bits left in!

Can you stomach the *sick* side of science? With Horrible Science you'll find out some truly gruesome facts. Fearsome fact files and curious quizzes, teacher tests and crazy cartoons have each title oozing with info!

Coming soon:

Ugly Bugs by Nick Arnold
Why do flies throw up on your tea? The insect world put underneath the magnifying glass.

Blood, bones and body bits by Nick Arnold
What happens when a boil bursts? The human body goes under the scalpel.

Look out for:

Comical chemicals by Nick Arnold
Which chemical was first found in caterpillar droppings? The explosive world of brews and potions revealed.

Evolve or Die! by Phil Gates
How did dinosaurs die? Step into the past and follow the scary fight for survival.

Science has never been so horrible!